GODS, HEROES, AND PHILOSOPHERS

GODS, HEROES, AND PHILOSOPHERS

A Celebration of All Things Greek

Christopher Bonanos

For Thalia —

CITADEL PRESS
Kensington Publishing Corp.
www.kensingtonbooks.com

CITADEL PRESS BOOKS are published by

Kensington Publishing Corp.
850 Third Avenue
New York, NY 10022

Copyright © 2005 Christopher Bonanos

All Kensington titles, imprints, and distributed lines are available at special quantity discounts for bulk purchases for sales promotions, premiums, fund-raising, educational, or institutional use. Special book excerpts or customized printings can also be created to fit specific needs. For details, write or phone the office of the Kensington special sales manager: Kensington Publishing Corp., 850 Third Avenue, New York, NY 10022, attn: Special Sales Department; phone: 1-800-221-2647.

CITADEL PRESS and the Citadel logo are Reg. U.S. Pat. & TM Off.

First Printing: November 2005

10 9 8 7 6 5 4 3 2 1

Printed in the United States of America

Library of Congress Control Number: 2005928511

ISBN 0-8065-2674-2

To Mom and Dad
S'agapo

Contents

Acknowledgments

Special thanks to Anastasia Rubis, who called me in at the start of this project and was generous and graceful when our plans diverged.

Doubly special thanks to Katherine Lumb, for tolerating a writer's cranky distraction for months.

And love and gratitude to Costandino, Costandina, Panagiotis, Argyris, and Agathoniki. Because they left Greece long ago, I am able to lead a very different life from theirs and return on my own terms. For that, I am immeasurably grateful.

PART I

FOOD

Roast Lamb

Certainly, Greeks are not the only ones who get a great deal of pleasure out of lamb. In India, it goes into the tandoor oven; in Mongolia, into sizzling oil; in Ireland and France, into the stewpot. But the Greek affection for lamb is singular. Slow-cooked on a rotating spit or roasted in the oven and then served with lemony roasted potatoes, orzo, or rice, a leg of lamb is the fundamental special-occasion dinner for Greeks all over the world. A solid dose of garlic is customary; so, unfortunately, is a tendency to overcook it. (Careful Greek chefs have learned, slowly, that leaving the lamb pink at its center improves the flavor and texture immeasurably.)

Today, of course, one can order a leg of lamb at any time of the year and roast it without much fuss. But in the age before easy transportation and refrigeration, the serving of a spring lamb was an extraordinarily special event. Sheep in the mountains of Greece bear their young at the end of the winter, and the lambs are ready for the market just in time for Easter, the most important day in the Greek Orthodox religion and the biggest event on the Greek calendar. (Rural families raised their own lambs; city families would buy them.) In the region of mainland Greece known as Roumeli, where much of the country's livestock is raised, roasting lambs on spits line the streets for the holiday, and you can probably imagine for yourself right now just how good it smells. (Milos, an excellent restaurant in New York City, sets up a fire pit with a rotisserie on the sidewalk every Easter and roasts several lambs outside. It's a striking sight—this primitive-looking arrangement on a Manhattan sidewalk—and the wafting scent is excellent for business.)

The Easter feast is of course celebratory, but it is also extremely practical. The holiday follows forty days of Lenten fasting from meat and animal products. For a hardworking farm family coming out of winter, that was a significant hardship—and when it came time to break the fast, they were surely not about to give up one scrap of protein. As a result, *everything* from that animal was used. To this day, the first food with which one breaks the Lenten fast is a hearty soup, made from the liver and other innards of the lamb, called *magheritsa*. It's served in the early hours of the morning, as the faithful return home from the midnight mass commemorating the Resurrection. Other parts of the animal go into sausages called *kokkoretsi*, into meatballs called *keftedes*, into stuffed cabbage, and onto skewers for *souvlaki*. Nothing is wasted—and it's all tasty.

Feta Cheese

Greece produces a lot of sheep and goats, and therefore a lot of cheese. There's halloumi, the smelly, tangy white cheese that's a signature product of the island of Cyprus. There's kasseri, an aged semisoft cheese, made in large wheels, that's a bit like provolone. There's graviera, a rather hard, sweet, mild cheese along the lines of Romano. But none of them—and perhaps no Greek food—is as well known as feta.

It's made from sheep's, goat's, or cow's milk, or sometimes a mixture thereof, and is rather heavily salted. There have been endless arguments over which milk is authentic, but all three have their regions and devotees. (If you're used to the American version, which is usually made with cow's milk, imported fetas will seem tangier and stinkier.) Though many different parts of Greece produce feta, it's chiefly associated with the mountains of mainland Greece and the Peloponnese peninsula. Today enormous factories crank out tons of feta every day, but the best remains artisanally made in small operations that age it in wooden barrels or small baskets. (A special tip of the hat here to the regional variety called "feta Dodonis," impressed with a capital delta monogram—Δ—and a bit creamier and less salty than the usual.) Nothing else dresses up a fresh salad or a plate of olives quite the same way. In violation of the Italian custom by which cheese rarely appears in the same dish with seafood, feta mixes well with shrimp, especially in a tomatoey shrimp stew that's a popular taverna item. In a few regions, some Greeks even dry their feta to make a hard aged cheese, though it's far less popular than the fresh variety; it's a throwback to the days before refrigeration, when drying for winter preservation was a necessity.

It may surprise some readers to learn that feta comes from all over Europe. There are French fetas, Bulgarian fetas, German fetas, and Danish fetas. (There's even a passable Wisconsin feta.) But its identity is so distinctively Hellenic that, after much wrangling, Greece in 2002 persuaded the European Union to regulate use of the name. To call their cheese "feta," producers have to be located only in specific regions of Greece, omit preservatives and antibiotics, and age their product a full two months under refrigeration. Cheese makers outside Greece have been given five years to come up with a new name for their product or stop selling it. The ruling looks particularly tough for the Danish feta industry, which has been operating for seventy-five years and is quite successful; on the other hand, archaeologists have evidence that the Greeks had a two-thousand-year head start.

The Greek Diner

Why are so many diners owned by Greeks? It's certainly a peculiar quirk of Americana: after all, there's nothing inherently Hellenic about slinging omelets and burgers. The numbers, however, don't lie. There are so many Greek restaurants in the United States that they even have their own magazine called *Estiator*, the Greek word for "restaurateur." Nobody knows exactly how many Greek-owned diners there are in the United States, but the total is surely in the thousands; one purchasing co-op that's limited to the New York City and northern New Jersey area has four hundred members. (By the way, what you call these places varies with local custom: for example, they're coffee shops in New York, but diners in the suburbs.)

These restaurants are often overlooked by the white-tablecloth set, but they serve a vital function. For one thing, many are open eighteen, twenty, or even twenty-four hours a day. That means that travelers can always get something to eat, that blue-collar workers coming off a shift at 2 A.M. can have a late dinner, and that weary college students coming off an all-nighter can have a bite and several cups of coffee before their exams. Moreover, their menus make up in variety and quantity what they may lack in refinement. On the typical diner menu, you'll find breakfast foods such as pancakes and waffles and dozens of omelets, a full deli-sandwich menu, burgers, pastas, soups, salads, a huge list of drinks, and a ridiculous number of pies, cakes, and other pastries. Very often, there'll be a few pages of the menu devoted to more elaborate cooking, like breast of veal or chicken Kiev. Usually there's also a Greek menu, incorporating a few baked dishes, like spanakopita, and a couple of desserts, like rice pudding. Sometimes it's excellent, sometimes not so great—but the diner's always there, the food's usually cheap, and the portions are huge.

But why so many Greeks? It seems to have happened this way: During the great wave of Mediterranean immigration to the United States, in the first two decades of the twentieth century, the Greeks who came over took whatever jobs they knew how to fill. For those who'd worked in the Greek shipping industry, that often meant dishwashing and kitchen work, since they'd picked up similar skills on board. These guys were tough and determined to make a good living, in large part so they could send money home. These men would sock away every spare penny, and after a couple of decades of scrubbing dishes, maybe rising to line cook along the way, they'd strike out on their own. What they knew how to do was run a restaurant—and if the Greeks we know today are any guide, they probably grumbled that they could do it better than the old boss could do.

To do that, however, the new owners would need kitchen help. Meanwhile, their cousins, brothers, and friends back home, who'd been hearing about their relatives' success in the United States and had seen money coming in the mail, wanted to join them. So the first wave of immigrants would sponsor the new wave—who would in turn spend a decade washing dishes, saving money, and plotting to open their own places. A couple of generations of this cycle, and the country was blanketed with Greek coffee shops, especially in the big northeastern and midwestern cities.

In 1975, *Saturday Night Live* immortalized one particular example of the breed. The new NBC show had imported a number of its cast and writers from Chicago's Second City comedy troupe, and one fellow, named Don Novello, wrote a silly sketch based on a well-known greasy spoon in the basement of the *Chicago Tribune* building called the Billy Goat Tavern. The owner, Bill Sianis, was known for his extremely limited menu, and John Belushi—another Chicago transplant—knew the role well. (Belushi's Albanian father had owned a couple of restaurants himself.) It took just three minutes of Belushi rattling off orders in the role of Pete Dionasopolis, manager of the Olympia Café, before "cheeseburger-cheeseburger-cheeseburger! No fries—*cheeps!* No Coke—*Pepsi!*" became shorthand for an entire class of restaurants and their Hellenic owners. A sample of the dialogue:

FEMALE CUSTOMER: Is he your brother?
PETE DIONASOPOLIS: *(pointing to guy at grill)* Him? No. My brother, Mike, he's in the back. George, he's my first cousin, but I treat him

like a brother. Sandy, she's my second cousin, but I treat her like a first cousin. Him . . . *(points to Niko)* . . . He's my third cousin, but I treat him like a fourth cousin, because he's *vlahos*. You know what that means? *Stupid. (Phone rings; Pete picks it up.)* Hello, Olympia Restaurant. That to go? Cheeseburger, cheeseburger, cheeseburger, cheeseburger. . . . No, no fries—chips. Four chips? Pepsi—no Coke. No orange. No grape. Pepsi. Four Pepsi! Okay, ten minutes.

It's pretty funny in print, but hilarious on-screen, and even more so with a Greek accent.

Greek Salad

Sad but true: the Greek salad as we know it in the United States isn't particularly Greek at all. The United States has a long history of creating dishes that evoke the cuisines of other cultures without actually being of those cultures, and the Greek salad is one of them. (Chow mein, for example, has almost nothing to do with China, and French dressing is about as Gallic as a Chevrolet.) The salads on a menu in Greece are usually made of tomatoes and cucumbers, lightly dressed with oil and lemon and a healthy dose of sea salt. Some salads also incorporate lightly cooked vegetables, like potatoes. Others add cheese; still others incorporate fresh herbs. They are often part of the light meal eaten at the end of the workday, before an evening out, and long before the late dinner customary in Mediterranean countries.

The Greek salad Americans know, on the other hand, is a great big basket of produce. It's usually based on lettuce, and a lot of it, that's tossed with whatever else the restaurateur seems to like, including, at the barest minimum, tomatoes, cucumbers, olives, shredded carrots, and red onions. The dressing is usually a mix of herb-flecked oil and red wine vinegar. The whole thing is crowned with feta, either in crumbles or in a solid block atop the pile of vegetables. (And although it may not be very Greek, it's very good, at least when the vegetables are fresh.)

Interestingly, the American tourists who began flocking to Greece in the 1960s came with expectations, perhaps honed in their local diners. They arrived in Athens cafés and island tavernas expecting a Greek salad and were quite confused when the restaurateurs knew of no such thing. But those restaurant guys know how to keep a customer happy, and if you go to Greece today, many menus—especially in areas frequented by tourists—list something called a "farm salad" on their menus. The camera-toting folks sit down with their guidebooks, place their orders, and declare the result "the best Greek salad I've ever had." It probably is, because Greek summer produce is excellent. Besides, they're eating the atmosphere as much as they are the tomatoes.

Yogurt

In America, yogurt is thought of almost as a medicine: a healthy food that takes the place of something really tasty, like a bowl of pudding. (In the versions that are commonly sold in the supermarket, the health benefits are often lost in the sugary stuff at the bottom. In fact, you may as well have a slice of banana cream pie, but never mind.) In Greece, however, nothing about yogurt carries even a hint of asceticism or self-denial. It's simply a rich, satisfying ingredient, much like a good cheese or the best heavy cream, and it has been so for thousands of years. This versatile food is an accidental discovery of a nameless ancient shepherd whose goatskin pouch of milk spoiled in a particularly tasty way, making it one of the world's oldest prepared foods.

The difference in attitude may be because there's a difference in the yogurt itself: the yogurt Greeks eat is very different from what comes in those little plastic Dannon cups. For one thing, it's full-fat yogurt. It can contain up to 9 percent butterfat, nearly as much as ice cream and about three times as much as American low-fat yogurt. (About the nonfat variety—well, it's good for you, and let's leave it at that.) That extra richness balances the tang of the yogurt's culture and makes it velvety on the tongue. Drizzled with honey and a sprinkling of chopped nuts, it's among the greatest of Greek desserts. Some diners also top it with a dollop of the sweetened, cooked fruit known as spoon sweets, or *glyko*—essentially, nice chunky preserves.

It's also the key ingredient in many dishes. Tzatziki, for example, is a mixture of yogurt with chopped cucumber, seasoned with a heavy dose of garlic and herbs, that's often served as an appetizer. It's especially welcome with spicy food, Greek or otherwise, because it cools down the palate so well. (A tip to the cook in your household: set the yogurt to drain through a fine strainer for several hours before you make the tzatziki, and it becomes thicker and even more luscious.)

Greeks in America have often had to make their own yogurt if they wanted the real McCoy, because it's not widely sold here. But that may be changing. A European company called Fage (Greek for "eat") has expanded Stateside and has begun selling an authentic full-fat Greek-style product under the brand name Total Yogurt. It's become a rather trendy item in New York City; it's sold in several different packages, the most distinctive of which is a single-serving plastic tub with a little container of honey attached. Even if you're having a hurried workday lunch at your desk, it's a minor treasure: you pour the honey over the yogurt, find a spoon, and pretend you're in Mykonos. Against all odds, this most old-fashioned food is at the crest of a trend, yet again.

Phyllo

There isn't much to making phyllo dough, besides a whole lot of patience and a big rolling pin. Mix water, flour, a little oil, and salt; knead the mixture till it's smooth, break off a lemon-sized hunk, and roll it out, endlessly, until it's bigger than a pizza and as thin as you can possibly get it. (Hence the name: phyllo means "leaf," as in the page of a book as well as on a tree.) Most modern cooks don't bother with making their own, preferring to buy frozen phyllo in the supermarket. When unwrapped, it looks somewhat blah, like a hank of rolled-up tissue paper, and if you leave it out on the counter for half an hour, it dries up and becomes impossible to handle.

But if there's no secret to phyllo, there most definitely is something special about the food based on it. Hundreds of Greek dishes call for this versatile pastry, which has roots going back at least two thousand years. (It's often indicated by the word "pita," meaning "pie," in a dish's name.) The key is in the assembly: the Greek chef laboriously layers those thin leaves of dough, brushing each with a teaspoon or so of melted butter. (A recipe will easily call for twenty sheets, and occasionally even more.) In the oven, the layers wrinkle slightly and separate as they turn golden brown. The result—when all goes correctly in the kitchen—is an unbelievable crispy flakiness, and pastry that shatters when you bite into it.

Spanakopita, that staple of Greek church suppers and diner menus, may be the best-known phyllo-based dish. A shell of layered, buttered phyllo sheets lines a pan, which is filled with a mixture of cooked spinach, feta, seasonings, and whatever other ingredients the cook's grandmother told her never to leave out. Another several layers of phyllo go on top, and you bake the whole dish and then slice it into squares that even some spinach-phobic children will tolerate. Alternatively, one can make little individual spanakopita triangles, wrapping a strip of phyllo around the filling, as one would fold a flag for presentation. These little puffs are usually served as appetizers, or as one of the world's greatest cocktail-party snacks.

The other much-loved phyllo dish is baklava. Found all over the Middle East in various forms, the Greek refinement of using phyllo rather than a piecrust-like dough renders it something extraordinary. The dough layers are interleaved with crushed, sweetened walnuts, after which the whole construction is doused in sugar syrup. It's a very sticky dessert, and on its own it can be a little too sweet for some palates—but add a cup of coffee, and the Greek ideal of balance and moderation is restored.

Moussaka

In many Greek American households, moussaka is the great test of a first-time visitor's savviness. The guest does not have to prepare it or compliment it or even like it—he or she simply has to know how to pronounce it. Greeks know that the accent goes on the final syllable, making it mous-sa-KAH; everyone else has an unerring knack for saying mous-SAK-ka. (And woe to them.)

Regardless of how you say it, it is a staple of the Greek kitchen, especially in the islands. Moussaka is a layered baked dish that takes as many forms as there are cooks, but the basic ingredients are eggplant, tomatoes, and ground lamb or beef, with a creamy white sauce, like the French béchamel, to top it all off. Here and there, zucchini replaces the eggplant, and a bread-crumb crust replaces the white sauce. Potatoes make guest appearances in some regional moussakas as well.

It's generally believed to have come to Greece via the Arab world, and versions of it pop up in Turkey and Lebanon; a thirteenth-century Arabic cookbook has a recipe that's quite recognizable as moussaka, though it lacks the top crust. Several dishes from around the Arab world also have similar names, though not all of them seem to have much in common with the Greek one. An ancient dish from the eastern Mediterranean is called "musakhkhan," for example, and the food historian Clifford Wright has proposed that it's an ancestor of moussaka, though the dishes have evolved to share little beyond that they're both meaty casseroles.

Today it's probably the most distinctively Hellenic dish of all, one that appears on virtually every Greek menu and in nearly every Greek cookbook. Unfortunately, it's often represented in heavy, greasy versions that don't do it justice. The eggplant is customarily sautéed in a skillet before the casserole is assembled, and if there's a bit too much oil in that pan, the vegetables soak it up and transfer the grease to the finished dish. In a careful chef's hands, however, it is a magnificent meal— warming and comforting on cold winter nights and remarkably unheavy as a summer dinner when the eggplants and tomatoes are at their best. Pronounce it right to your Greek host, and you'll doubtless get a second helping. Maybe a third too. And a big piece wrapped up for lunch tomorrow.

Pastitsio

Pastitsio is perhaps not as well known as the other great Greek casserole dish, moussaka. And it's certainly less familiar to most Americans than lasagna, baked ziti, or several other Italian baked casseroles. But it's a dish that deserves greater popularity than it has, and one that can survive more abuse than almost any. As has often been said about pizza, "When it's good, it's great; when it's bad, it's still pretty good."

A pastitsio is a rather messy dish, built with layers of a meaty tomato sauce, tubular pasta, such as ziti or penne, and a pillowy béchamel sauce to cap it all off. (Many recipes call for two sauces: one thin one to coat the pasta and one thick one to cover the top.) The meat sauce often incorporates red wine, and grated cheese and beaten eggs often enrich the whole mixture, which is then baked till it's bubbly and comforting. Many chefs include heavy doses of seasonings such as cinnamon and chopped herbs. (The excellent food writer Diane Kochilas has noted that creamy dishes made with egg pasta are common to shepherd communities, where dairy products were always readily available. Although

Kochilas doesn't include a pastitsio in her authoritative book *The Glorious Foods of Greece*—the volume sticks to less well-known regional cuisines—she does mention a macaroni pie that looks a bit like a pastitsio without the meat.)

It's popular taverna food—rarely does one run across a neighborhood menu in Greece without a pastitsio on it—and it's a durable, tasty entrant at church festivals and other gatherings. Pastitsio gains particular favor around February, when one often makes it for the week leading up to Lent and serves it on the Sunday of Apokreos, which is the last Sunday on which the faithful can eat meat. It's no coincidence that during this very cold portion of the year, a sturdy, rich dinner is exactly what's called for.

Souvlaki and Gyros

As in so many matters, the Turks and Greeks duel over which came first: the Greek souvlaki or the Turkish shish kebab. (One could argue that neither did: grilling meat on a stick over a fire is pretty basic and was probably invented everywhere, independently, at one time or another.) The Turks say their soldiers used their swords to roast their dinner, and the Greeks counter with Byzantine art showing very familiar-looking skewers over a fire. But the Greeks probably win, if only because they can cite one of history's greatest writers in their favor. In Homer's *Odyssey*, King Nestor recalls a banquet scene (rendered here by the translator Robert Fagles):

> *There sat Nestor among his sons as friends around them*
> *decked the banquet, roasted meats and skewered strips for broiling.*

Regardless of their origins, souvlakia have become popular street food throughout the world because they're easy to prepare almost anywhere and can be sold and nibbled on while you're walking. (The name, by the way, comes from the Greek *souvla*, meaning a spit or skewer.) They're at their best when the meat has been marinated in yogurt, herbed olive oil, or a similar preparation so that it doesn't dry out over the coals.

If souvlaki is noble and ancient, the gyro is its sloppy, charming nephew. It's also a dish of debated origins and may owe its origins to the Turks, who call it a "doner kebab," or the Arabs, who call it "shawarma." The gyro is fundamentally a twentieth-century product, a sandwich that serves much the same function, in the Mediterranean world, as a burger does here—quick, inexpensive, filling. No matter who's making it or naming it, however, a gyro is made with meat sliced off a vertical rotisserie that's heated from the sides. The meat varies, but it's most often lamb, pounded thin and pressed down on the spit, so that by the time it's done, it's pressed almost into a meatloaf-like solid. (In fact, the versions often served at inferior restaurants use a compressed, heavily seasoned cylinder of meat rather than the traditional cuts, to simplify cooking and slicing. It's easy on the chef, but it's pretty bad from the diner's point of view.) A few thin pieces come off the spit and are plopped into a waiting pita, then topped with a handful of diced tomatoes, perhaps some greens, and a dollop of tzatziki, which is especially cool and tasty when the meat's hot and well-done. If it's made correctly, everything runs down your arms when you're eating it. A proper gyro is messy street food at its best.

Octopus and Kalamari

One can argue over whether Greeks can call these wriggly, funny-looking creatures a part of their own cuisine. Every country facing the Mediterranean (Italy, France, Spain, Tunisia) has rendered them one tasty way or another. But their ubiquity on taverna menus makes them inherently part of Hellenic culture, and octopus, in particular, seems more popular in Greece than anywhere. (And no wonder: the very words *octa podi*, "eight feet," are Greek.) Besides, a striking number of ancient images show a big-eyed octopus being caught or celebrated; for example, a vase from 1500 B.C. is covered with legs and tentacles and looks like one of the creatures is about to consume it. Plentiful and cheap, squid was available even to poorer Greeks—at least those in the islands—and was prepared in many, many ways. It was often boiled, though fried squid gets a mention in a play by Aristophanes.

In Greece today, octopus is most often marinated and grilled, and served in a vinegary sauce and not much more, to let its flavor come out. Although Americans, uncomfortable with its tentacles and suckers, often avoid it on menus, adventurous diners can be quickly converted by the meaty, mild flavor of the white flesh, especially when it's a bit charred and crunchy on the outside. It's often served during Lent, when meat is prohibited. Interestingly, it has to be pounded vigorously before it's cooked, to break down the fibers and render it tender to the bite; culinary lore has it that one American chef puts his octopus in a stout bag and drives over it with his Jeep.

As for squid, they're among the best candidates for deep-frying that there is. Cut into rings or strips and lightly coated with flour or crumbs, it's crunchy and (when carefully prepared) remarkably light. Squid are also often stuffed, especially with rice, or stewed in various preparations. Undercooked or badly overcooked squid are, true to their unfortunate reputation, like rubber. But as long as they're cooked with care, they're as tender and delicious as shrimp.

Avgolemono

One cannot begin talking about avgolemono without a discussion of lemons. There are Greeks who eat virtually nothing—fish or fowl, vegetable or animal—without adding a healthy squeeze of lemon juice on top. Especially in the south of Greece and in Cyprus, where citrus is grown, lemons find their way into nearly every meal. Along with olive oil and salt, lemon juice is simply a basic condiment.

Hence, the popularity of avgolemono, which is a thick mixture of eggs, lemon juice, and, usually, chicken broth. (The word itself is a recipe: *avgo* means "egg," and *lemono* you can probably figure out for yourself.) It takes a little practice to make avgolemono, because the combination of acidic lemon juice and hot stock tends to curdle the eggs; very gentle heat plus some handiwork with a whisk is required to keep everything smooth and creamy. Once the basic mixture is assembled, avgolemono can take a couple of forms: With a modest bit of stock, it's a sauce meant to be poured over lamb, chicken, or vegetables. The meatballs called *keftedes*, swimming in a pool of avgolemono, are especially tasty. (For a major treat, try it over an artichoke sometime.) Or thinned out with more chicken stock and thickened up again with a restrained dose of rice or small pasta, like orzo, it's a satisfying soup, memorable as much for its pretty yellow color as for its taste.

This may be my own Hellenic chauvinism talking, but I consider it the best chicken soup there is, and maybe the best soup of any kind. (As a college student, I very nearly lived on the stuff, and my non-Greek roommates, quick converts all, learned to make it for themselves.) The flavors and textures are in perfect balance—the acid in the lemon juice gives an edge to the richness of the eggs and chicken, and the starch from the rice gives it just the right amount of body. It thickens up in the refrigerator, making it even better the second day. Anyone who thinks Jewish grandmothers have a monopoly on chicken soup hasn't been to a Greek house.

Olives and Olive Oil

The ancients believed that olives were a gift from the goddess Athena herself—that her thrown spear struck a rock atop the Acropolis and sprouted into an olive tree. It's a powerful image, and even more so when one realizes its resonance in the Greek mind. Much of Greece's land is arid and hot, and centuries of human habitation have taken their toll on some of its farmland, giving the Greek farmer a tough job. So a tree that bears fruit out of bad, rocky soil must quite literally have been a lifesaver. Little wonder it was considered divine. Homer called olive oil "liquid gold," and Solon, the lawmaker who wrote the first constitution of Athens, declared it the city-state's only legal export. The winning athletes at the ancient Olympic Games received not medals but crowns of olive boughs, and the olive branch carried forth as a peace offering survives, metaphorically, to the present day.

In a more earthly, practical sense, it's also a useful crop, for the simple reason that olives are both food and raw material. The fruits themselves are familiar to everyone; the most distinctively Greek variety of olives is from Kalamata. They are picked quite carefully, often by hand so that they don't get soiled or bruised. (Modern machines shake the trees, catching the fruit in nets so it doesn't hit the ground.) Though many olives are a dull green—of course they are! The color's called olive green!—Kalamata olives are a muddy purplish black. (By the way, olives are inedible before they're cured in a strong salt brine for at least a few weeks. If you do bite into a raw one, you'll find it terribly bitter and rock-hard.) They make their way into every kind of cooking, but spend plenty of time on their own. It's almost impossible to sit down in a Greek house, let alone get through a meal, without being offered a plate of olives.

But as good as it may be to eat, the real value of the olive, ancient and modern, comes when it is pressed in a device called a *liotrivia*. Under the pressure of heavy stones, the fruit exudes oil that is greener and more substantial than that of most fruits or seeds, and far more flavorful. The first pressing produces oil with the most body and character of all. Called "extra-virgin olive oil," it's prized for culinary uses where its flavor is detectable, especially in salad dressings. (And before you say anything, no more extra-virgin jokes, please.) Subsequent pressings, for which the olive pulp is sometimes heated, make oil that's lighter, milder, and less expensive. This product, usually sold as "pure olive oil"—no virgins here—is useful for less exalted tasks like deep-frying, although it's not the best for recipes that depend on the oil's flavor, such as salad dressing. The ancients even burned it in their lamps, though olive oil's low smoke point must have meant the light was not without its drawbacks.

Greeks consume more olive oil per capita than any other population, but they export a lot of what they produce, which totals 400,000 tons per year. That's enough to place the country among the top producers in the world. As any proud Greek will tell you, it's also a premium product. The better Greek olive oils hold their own against those from Italy, California, Spain, and everywhere else and are often great bargains.

Ouzo and Meze

In one popular American conception, a raucous Greek party isn't complete until mustachioed men start smashing plates against the bricks of the fireplace, yelling *"Opa! Opa!"* It's a durable image, promoted in restaurants and tourist brochures for generations, and it's mostly just that: an image. (If nothing else, Greeks are savvy about business, and plates aren't cheap.) But if the stereotype has any currency whatsoever, we blame ouzo. The sweet anise-flavored liqueur, beloved of café patrons, has rendered some drinkers ready and able to shatter anything that falls into their hands.

Ouzo is a distilled spirit, like whiskey or gin. Most famously associated with the island of Lesvos, it's usually 40 to 45 percent alcohol and flavored with anise oil and a few herbs. It's furiously strong, all the more so because its sweetness sometimes hides its potency. Although ouzo is often drunk straight, in small glasses, many moderate imbibers add a little bit of water to make it less harsh. Doing so also has a curious chemical effect: the clear liqueur turns cloudy and bright white.

The real way to moderate ouzo's effects, however, is to consume it the way nature—or at least the Greeks—intended. A Greek café typically has a varied menu of small dishes, called "meze" (plural: mezedes), meant to be ordered a few at a time with drinks, a little like the Spanish bar food known as tapas. Mezedes come in a breathtaking variety, drawn from every cuisine in Europe and the Middle East—plates of stuffed or grilled vegetables, small salads, sausages, grilled meat, crispfried little fish, slow-cooked fava beans, and literally hundreds of other options. Spreads, such as taramosalata and tzatziki, are staples of the meze table, in part because they accompany the bread that is so basic to a Greek meal.

To Americans, they look a lot like appetizers, but mezedes do not precede a meal. They are part of the end-of-the-workday repast that fuels an Athenian evening out, in a ritual that often depends on the waiter's selection of dishes as much as the diner's. Conversation is king at the meze table; also vital is the liveliness of the group as a whole, as people reach across the table for their selections, refresh each other's drinks, argue, laugh, and in general carry on in a manner that—all around the Mediterranean, and especially in Greece—a great many people consider the epitome of a well-lived life.

Vasilopeta

In the Orthodox Church, every day has its own saint, and on that day each year, everyone named for that saint receives cards and gifts. (In fact, until recently, name days were much more commonly celebrated among Greeks than birthdays.) January 1 is St. Basil's day, celebrated by everyone named Vassili or Vassiliki and memorializing a saint who was known for his kindnesses to the indigent. His story, by most accounts, centers on a particular miracle: Basil, assigned to collect taxes from the poor, had taken jewelry in payment. The governor (either out of sympathy or because he'd found money elsewhere) allowed Basil to return the jewelry to its owners—but Basil no longer knew which piece had come from whom. He asked for divine guidance, baked each item into a loaf of bread, distributed the loaves to the citizens—and, in the miracle for which he's sanctified, returned the correct jewelry to each taxpayer.

Which brings us to the *vasilopeta*—literally "Basil's cake." Every year, on New Year's Day, Greeks gather for a feast that ends with a special dessert. It's a cake—sometimes a bread, depending on where your grandmother's from—which has had a coin dropped into its batter before baking. The ranking member of the household, or a prominent visitor, does the cutting; the first piece is set aside for St. Basil himself, and the second for Christ. Subsequent slices are distributed in a strict order, from the most venerable member of the family down to the youngest. Someone, of course, gets the coin buried in the cake, and that person is said to have good luck and prosperity for the full year to come. Tradition calls for a gold coin, but that's pretty much fallen by the wayside; when a silver coin is used, it comes out black with tarnish from its immersion into the damp batter. St. Basil's slice of the cake is given to a needy resident of the neighborhood, to honor Basil's commitment to the poor. (Although this is the best-known Greek tradition on January 1, it's not the only one. Some families break a pomegranate over the house's threshold on New Year's Day, and if it's ripe and juicy inside, it portends an excellent year.) Some historians say that the Orthodox tradition derives from the even older practices of pre-Christian Greeks, who made offerings to the gods of valuables baked into their breads.

The recipes vary greatly from region to region and from family to family. Some are actual breads, made from risen yeast doughs. On the island of Rhodes, *vasilopeta* is often a cake, sweetened with orange juice and topped with almonds. On Chios, where the pine resin known as *masticha*—the flavoring in the Greek wine retsina—is common, it's added to the *vasilopeta*. Still other versions are made with phyllo dough, and various cooks flavor their cakes with everything from pistachio nuts to cinnamon. The only constant is the coin—and the timing because it's served and cut just after midnight, bringing in the New Year, as it has for centuries.

Dolmades

The stuff inside a dolma (stuffed grape leaf) is relatively unremarkable food. Rice, some herbs, a bit of oil, and maybe a little ground meat, all cooked together. You could stuff a turkey or a pork chop or a cabbage with it, and nobody would raise an eyebrow. But on the outside, dolmades are unique because they are wrapped with grape leaves. We can't identify the Greek grower of grapes (or, admittedly, Turk or Arab; it's unclear where dolmades got their start) who one day eyeballed his vine, pulled off a big tough leaf, and thought to cure it, rendering it pliable and soft and edible. One assumes that, like so many old-world chefs, he or she was looking to use simply everything possible—why should those big dramatic leaves go to waste, after all? But regardless of his or her motivation, that unnamed chef is responsible for a distinctive and versatile food item that few Greeks will fail to recognize. Some Mediterranean chefs also wrap other things in grape leaves—whole fish, for example, or occasionally even small birds, for roasting.

But back to the dolmades, which, because they're made all over the

Middle East, have developed hundreds of small local variations. In Macedonia and Thrace, raisins and pine nuts work their way into the stuffing. Other local variants call for the inclusion of herbs, such as coriander and mint, or currants or a dollop of tomato or *avgolemono* sauce over the top. Some are meaty; some are vegetarian. In recent years, dolmades have gained their fame in part because they are readily available almost anywhere in cans. Though they lack much of the fresh character of homemade ones, the tinned substitute is still pretty tasty. At an American picnic, dolmades would certainly be the talk of any crowd that's accustomed to just potato salad. That may be why they're such a staple among American caterers—plus the fact that they're perfect and easy-to-handle finger food. And here's a shortcut for your next cocktail party, one that I have employed often: the canned dolmades get much tastier when they're drained of their oil and doused in fresh lemon juice. Try this, and if your guests ooh and aah and ask you about them, tell everyone you "prepared" them yourself.

Grapes, Wine, and Retsina

Eventually, even the most devout Hellenophile has to admit that the Greeks didn't invent everything. Winemaking, it appears, long predates the rise of Greece; in fact, its provenance goes back further than anyone can tell. (The first hard evidence that we have is from Persia.) In fact, it's somewhat likely that nobody invented wine, per se—that some grapes probably fermented by accident somewhere and produced a flavor that people liked. But we can say with assurance that the Greeks *loved* their wine. The Greek climate grows good wine grapes, and the ancient Greeks produced tons of it for their own use and for export, building a shipping business around its distribution. They sent it everywhere they conquered, from Egypt to France, as the Romans did after them. They had special drinking cups of multiple shapes and sizes, many of which survive to this day, such as *kraters*, the large, elaborately decorated ceramic vessels in which the wine was diluted with water before serving. And the Greeks were excellent drinkers.

Every myth and every record of a festival seemingly includes a story of tippling; many, of course, center on Dionysus, god of wine. (He was also the god of theater, which may explain how actors began getting drunk at post-premiere parties.) One wonders what exactly ancient wine tasted like, as we can only guess from the vague surviving records. Some years ago, the French diver Jacques Cousteau pulled up a sealed amphora full of wine that had lain on the floor of the Mediterranean for two millennia and opened it up to pour himself a glass. Unfortunately, the contents had become indistinguishable from seawater.

The rise of Christian Greece did little to change the country's affection for wine—it's part of the ritual of communion in the Orthodox Church, and it's not a religion that prohibits taking a drink now and then. But the Turkish conquest of Greece was another story. Turkey, a Muslim country, is by no means friendly to alcohol consumption, and in any case, the conquered Greeks had more on their mind trying to survive the occupation than tending their vineyards. After Greece finally shook off the last of its Turkish rule early in the twentieth century, the wineries began improving again—yet Greek wine continued to have a mediocre reputation at best. Why? It seems that the wine business in Greece is centered on very small, carefully tended local vineyards, as it is in France. But whereas the French export a good portion of their best product to England, America, and beyond, the Greeks appear to have taken the opposite approach: they drink the good wine themselves and export the second-rate stuff, giving their product a lousy reputation overseas.

But the real reputation-killer was retsina. Retsina is a white wine, served chilled, that is infused with the sap of pine trees, called *masticha*. Some versions are strongly resinated, some are more mildly perfumed, but all carry the singular scent of a fresh-cut Christmas tree. It's a wine that some people like, and one that has plenty to recommend it: A cold glass of retsina with a plate of rich meaty cooking, such as a lamb stew with orzo, cuts through the salt and fat perfectly. It also goes very nicely with grilled fish, especially in the summertime, because it's so crisp. But the fact is, many people find it hard to get the stuff past their noses. Retsina is an acquired taste, and one that many people feel no need to acquire. (You hear it repeatedly: "That stuff tastes like a handful of pine needles.") The fact that the flavoring was often used to mask the flavor of cheap and inferior wine exacerbated the problem. And since many people had never experienced any other Greek wine, retsina's bad reputation unfairly turned a great many people off for a long time.

Only in the past decade or so has that begun to change for the better. The better Greek wineries, led by Boutari, have worked to improve their international profile, sending some of the good stuff overseas. They've put their better products into American restaurants and wine shops. They've also improved their wines to the point where they are competitive with those from the nearby winemaking countries like Italy. (In my own experience, the reds from Naoússa, in the north, are excellent, and the sweet dessert wine called Mavrodáphni is a particular treat.) And wine buyers in America and elsewhere are just beginning to take notice—not least because Greek wines remain relatively inexpensive, having (so far) avoided the price increases that have made the better French and California labels almost unattainable. If recent history is any guide, this is a good time to buy the best, sturdiest Greek wines you can find and get them into your cellar. If the prices go up, you'll be sitting on a minor treasure. If not, well, you can just drink up your investment. Either way, you win. Raise a glass and say, "*Eis iyian*"—the classic Greek toast.

Figs

The climate of Greece rather strictly limits what's grown there. The hot summers, generally arid climate, and rocky, often overworked soil can be tough on farmers. But the Greeks have made the most of what they can grow and have done so for a very long time. Ancient crops, such as almonds, wine grapes, and (of course) olives are basic to Greek agriculture. So it is with figs, one of the earliest cultivated fruits.

References to them abound in ancient literature. The biblical Garden of Eden had fig trees; it's even been postulated that the apple that tempted Eve was no apple at all but a fig. The asp that killed Cleopatra was brought to her in a basket of figs; Homer writes about them repeatedly. The Roman writer Pliny called them "restorative," adding that "they increase the strength of young people, preserve the elderly in better health, and make them look younger with fewer wrinkles." He wasn't alone in his belief—Roman literature refers to the fruit often and approvingly. And, of course, Renaissance sculptors and painters often used a fig leaf to cover up various bits of embarrassing anatomy—ironic, really, given that the juicy fruit is often thought of as particularly luscious and sensual.

Most of us encounter dried figs far more often than we do fresh ones, and there are a couple of reasons for that. For one thing, figs dehydrate well, turning flavorful and delicious and taking on a nice chewy texture. (That also may account for their prominence in the ancient world: a handful of dried figs must have been the best, sweetest thing an ancient shepherd could have possibly tasted on a dark, cold February day.) The Greek ones come mostly from Kalamata, where they're punched with small holes and strung, like beads, for storage. In fact, they're the rare fruit that begins to dry out while still on the tree, gradually dehydrating as part of the ripening process.

Fortunately, figs haven't really been bred for looks and transportability rather than flavor, like American tomatoes and apples have. Unfortunately, however, that means they don't travel well, and even if you can find them, the fruit that comes to market in the United States is often either tasteless or almost rotten. (If you happen to be near the growers, most of whom are in northern California, it's another story entirely, and you should take advantage of your unusual and excellent supply line.)

There is one other way to get excellent fresh figs in almost any part of the world: plant a tree yourself. Figs are not particularly demanding to grow, and it's not as uncommon a step as you might think. In Greek and Italian neighborhoods in the northeastern United States, they're common in front-yard and backyard gardens. At the first sign of cold in

October or November, the growers gently bundle up their trees, tying the branches inward, wrapping the plant in blankets, and placing a bucket over the top to keep the cold wind from drying them out. Come spring, the unwrapped trees bud on the old branches rather than starting from the ground. My own grandfather did this in his small Brooklyn backyard, right next to an elevated subway line, and his tree grew and bore for decades, at its peak producing a small bowl of sweet fruit every day during the summer. And a branch from that tree—carried on vacation to a relative's house in South Carolina, where the winters are mild, and casually stuck into the earth—became a huge shade tree as well.

Greek Coffee

Roast the beans dark, and grind them on the finest setting of your coffee grinder. For each person you wish to serve, place a heaping spoonful of the resultant powder into a small brass pot, along with a half-cup of water, a spoonful or two of sugar, and, if you're feeling exotic, a couple of cardamom pods. Bring to a boil, and watch the foam on top form and rise; when the froth rises to the point where it's about to boil over, quickly pull the pot off the heat. (Many people then bring it back to a boil twice more, out of tradition.) Let it stand for a minute to settle, and pour the liquid off into tiny demitasse cups, making sure that each drinker gets some of the foam.

The recipe above gives you the basics of Greek coffee, and it's something that's easy to make successfully, even on the first try. Often called "Turkish coffee"—though you'd be well advised not to use that term in a Greek restaurant, especially when the endless rivalry between Greece and Turkey flares up—drinking this beverage is the basic way to end a meal in Greece, and it's also a repeated ritual throughout the day. The small restaurants called *kafeníons,* where men and women sit, argue, and nibble for hours on end, are named for the stuff.

The amount of sugar varies with the drinker's taste. You can typically order your coffee in one of four ways: *skéttos* (no sugar), *métrios* (medium sweet), *glykos* (sweet), or *variglykos* (extra sweet). *Kafe métrios,* in particular, is the favorite of younger coffee drinkers, whereas older folks tend to order theirs sweeter.

The coffeepots, called *bríki,* are quite distinctive. They vary from one- to three-cup sizes to much larger versions to serve large groups. Most are brass; some are heavily decorated, and some are plain. But all have long handles, so you don't burn yourself over the fire, and all have the same distinctive shape: a bottom-heavy hourglass, with a wide base tapering to a small neck, topped by a wide-mouthed flaring lip. A specialized grinder makes an appearance in some houses as well. It's cylindrical, with a hand crank on top, and its burrs are very close together, allowing the coffee to be milled to a superfine powder. (Most electric grinders can't quite get it fine enough.)

That last fact is responsible for a peril that awaits the novice Greek coffee drinker. Your last sip should not—I repeat, *should not*—be tossed back with abandon, because the bottom of the cup contains half an inch of muddy sludge. Should you get this stuff on your tongue, you'll taste it for, roughly speaking, two days. It's fiercely bitter, gritty, and altogether nasty (many Greek restaurants serve a glass of water with their coffee, just in case). Leave it in the cup, and don't be tempted by that final one-half teaspoon of liquid. If there's an old-fashioned Greek woman at your table, you can ask her to read your fortune in the grounds, much as some cultures read tea leaves. She'll invert the cup on its saucer, swish it around a few times, and take a reading from the pattern on the inside of the demitasse. It may be a somewhat silly superstition, but if nothing else, it'll finish off your cup—and allow you to order another one.

PART II

PEOPLE

Maria Callas

Great sopranos enjoy special status in the classical-music world. Fans throw themselves at their feet, camp out in line for tickets to their shows, and trade hard-to-find recordings as religiously as any Grateful Dead fan. And there is no figure in opera with quite the cult following of Cecilia Sophia Anna Maria Kalogeropoulos, known to the world as Maria Callas. With each passing year, her legend becomes a little more burnished and refined. If great sopranos are rock stars, Callas is Elvis Presley—and led a life that was, if anything, even more colorful than that of the King.

Born in New York shortly after her Greek parents immigrated in 1923, Callas went to Greece for her conservatory training at the age of fourteen. By 1940, she'd made her debut in Athens, and over the next few years her name grew famous in Greece. In 1946, she auditioned for the Metropolitan Opera in New York and, depending on whose story you believe, either was rejected or turned down the secondary roles she was offered. Returning to Europe, she began to build a career, eventually making her debut in 1950 at La Scala, Milan's famed opera house, in the title role of Verdi's *Aïda*. Her reputation as a singer was blossoming, as was her reputation as a diva, and a troubled one at that. Like so many great singers, Callas had an operatic temperament in private as well as onstage. When she finally made her first appearance at the Metropolitan Opera in 1956, an ugly break with her mother had just become public, and she was met with weak applause when she made her entrance. It would have taken a spectacular performance to win over the New York crowd—and that's what she proceeded to deliver.

What was so great about Callas's voice? Operagoers say it was her supreme ability to express a part's demands through the notes rather than extraneous vocal gestures—no howls, no shrieks, just music. They add that she was an excellent actor, bringing far more to her roles than merely a voice. That aside, she brought an exotic beauty to the stage, particularly when midway through her career, she lost about 75 pounds. (Some of her detractors say that her weight loss ruined her voice—that she never sounded the same afterward—though most critics seem to agree her dieting had little to do with a decline that had already begun.)

In fact, her legend in part comes from the fact that her prime career was very brief. Though she sang into the 1970s, most agree that she should have retired much earlier. (Fans point to a dozen years of her recordings, on EMI Records from 1950 to 1962, as her greatest legacy and by far her best work.) Many of her later concerts and recordings were embarrassing for both her and her audiences; after one notorious performance in 1965, where she simply could not keep up with her costars, she collapsed after the final curtain. Other, similar humiliations bore down on her: an overdose of pills in 1970 that landed her in the hospital and a disastrous comeback tour in 1973 that left critics shaking their heads.

And, always, there was the story of her affair with Aristotle Onassis. The two met in 1959, around the time Callas divorced her husband and settled into a storied, stormy affair that lasted the rest of their lives. Onassis was dismissive of her art and rude to her in public; Callas, for her part, seemed eager both to please him and to be high-handedly dismissive at the same time. She found his endless philandering difficult to face, but tolerated his betrayals as a necessary part of his aggressive personality—that is, until he abruptly dumped her, without explanation, for the widowed Jacqueline Kennedy in 1968. Callas was furious and cut him out of her life. Yet, several years later, as Onassis and his wife grew distant, Callas took him back, perhaps platonically, perhaps not. What we do know is that Onassis's death in 1975 shattered her. Less than three years later, she was gone as well, dead of a heart attack in her Paris apartment, aged just 53, alone but for her housekeeper. Her ashes were scattered into the Aegean.

Melina Mercouri

When she died in 1994, the Greek American magazine *Odyssey* put her on the cover, of course, with a black-and-white glamour photo—no headline or eulogy, just one word: MELINA.

That single word was enough. Melina Mercouri, for many people, *was* Greece. On-screen and off, she represented everything people embrace about Mediterranean living: an ability to enjoy life, an uninhibited personal style, and, most of all, a vividness of spirit. Moreover, after she retired from movies, Mercouri did what she was clearly born to do. As a public official, she served as the worldwide public face for Greek culture, especially when it came to movies, music, or national heritage.

She was born in 1920 in Athens, the daughter of a Greek politician, and married young (and briefly) at twenty-one. Within a few years, she began to establish her reputation on the Greek stage, gaining attention for her roles with the National Theater and starring as Blanche DuBois in *A Streetcar Named Desire* in 1949. That in turn led to a screen career, beginning with the 1955 film *Stella*, directed by Michael Cacoyannis, who later became famous for his *Zorba the Greek*.

Though this work gave her some prominence, she was hardly an internationally famous figure—until 1960. That's when she starred in *Never on Sunday*, the film that made her a legend. Mercouri's turn as a vivacious prostitute in Piraeus, whose zest for life charmed audiences all over the world, made her career. It's a twist on *Pygmalion*, or *My Fair Lady*: her male companion decides that she needs to soak up some of Greece's highbrow culture, and she in turn—and inevitably!—loosens him up. Her performance overcame the hooker-with-a-heart-of-gold clichés of the part, and an Oscar nomination followed. Many people still say Mercouri should have won, although it wasn't her year (and it was Elizabeth Taylor's). But she did take home one prize: her French director and costar, Jules Dassin, who a few years later became her husband.

When the military junta seized power in Greece in 1967, Melina—always politically active—spoke out against the new government. She was promptly deported and spent the next few years in Paris, working on films and agitating for the generals' overthrow. Not long after democracy was restored to Greece in 1974, Melina made her triumphant return to Athens, not just as a citizen, but as an elected member of the new Greek parliament. Her popularity served her well, and in 1981, she rose to the post of Minister of Culture, becoming an activist for the return of the Parthenon marbles and the preservation of Greece's antiquities and heritage. Perhaps most important, though, was her role as an international ambassador for Greece. Because of her movie fame, she could get in to see any public official anywhere—and charm him or her senseless once she got through the door.

George Stephanopoulos

When George Stephanopoulos signed onto Bill Clinton's presidential campaign, he thought it was going to be a brief, interesting ride—"a terrific experience," he told an interviewer a decade later. "That this was a smart guy who was going to move the party a little bit, bring ideas into the campaign, and have a noble loss. Even if he got the nomination, George Bush looked unbeatable."

Of course, we all know what happened. Bush stumbled, Clinton ran one of the most effective campaigns in history, and by Election Day it was no contest. A look at the great documentary *The War Room* shows how they did it and especially shows that two aides to the candidate—Stephanopoulos and his colleague James Carville—were as responsible as any for the win. The duo figured out what recent Democratic campaigns had not: that quick responses to attacks were essential, especially if they came in ways that played to particular tendencies of the news media. (For example, the Clinton spin on any major story had to get to the networks by two-thirty in the afternoon, because that's when the evening news broadcasts fix most of their schedule.) Stephanopoulos also grew famous himself, partly because of his age (just thirty-one), partly because of his charm and ease on camera, and partly because of his looks. The campaign is said to have filled several file cabinets with love letters sent to George.

Though his access to political figures is nearly unmatched, Stephanopoulos hardly comes from a Washington, D.C., background. Stephanopoulos's father, Robert, is a Greek Orthodox priest, serving at the cathedral on Manhattan's Upper East Side; his mother, Nikki, is the public-relations director for the church's American archdiocese. (Their son has often spoken about the moral grounding of his upbringing, and it certainly served him in his career. Even through the scandals of the Clinton years, Stephanopoulos came out completely clean.) A degree from Columbia University and a Rhodes Scholarship at Oxford burnished his résumé.

After Clinton's election, Stephanopoulos served in several roles in the White House, usually as a senior advisor but also, briefly and unsuccessfully, as the president's press secretary. The political infighting of Washington took its toll, however, and Stephanopoulos left the White House soon after Clinton was reelected in 1996. His memoir *All Too Human,* published three years later, topped the best-seller list, and painted a vivid, well-written, and quite candid picture of the conflicts and stresses inherent in his earlier job.

What does a political media expert do after he's burned out on politics? In Stephanopoulos's case, the answer was to become a media figure himself. Soon after the success of his book, Stephanopoulos joined

ABC News as an analyst, becoming the first high-profile Greek American on a network since Ike Pappas appeared in the 1960s. Though some critics at the time suggested that he'd have a tough time being any kind of impartial journalist, he quickly acquitted himself and was successful enough that, in 2002, he succeeded the retiring David Brinkley as the host of the Sunday morning show *This Week*. Though he's had ups and downs in the ratings, he remains extremely well regarded. And every Greek American gets to feel a brief, happy moment of vicarious success once a week, when that ungainly name sprawls across the screen during the credits.

Costa-Gavras

Many filmmakers who let their political feelings filter into their work end up making strident and angry movies that are all but unwatchable. But Constantine Costa-Gavras—who has all but stopped using his first name in recent years—has never divorced his politics from his art yet has consistently managed to make entertaining films. For this he's taken home two Oscars and worldwide acclaim.

He may have been born a political fighter; in fact, his father was a key figure in the Greek resistance against the Nazi invaders during World War II. After a youth spent constantly watching American films, Costa-Gavras broke into the scene in the midsixties with a movie called *The Sleeping Car Murders*—which, unlike many European films of its day, unabashedly drew on Hollywood technique.

But he really came to international attention with a film called *Z*, released in 1969. Six years earlier, a professor at the University of Athens had been run down by a car in Salonika in a murder intended to look like an accident. The investigation turned up a major corruption scandal, leading to the election of George Papandreou, who was soon after thrown out of office by a military coup. This real-life story already sounds like a thriller, and in fact, a novelist named Vassili Vassilikos turned it into a novel, which became Costa-Gavras's film. The great Mikis Theororakis supplied the score, even though he was being held in Greece by the generals, under house arrest; some say his score was smuggled to France, where Costa-Gavras was making the film. (The director could not return to Greece, because of his radical politics, and shot the exterior scenes in Algeria.)

The film was a worldwide success, even in the United States, which was just waking up to international cinema. Hollywood gave Costa-Gavras its ultimate prize: the Oscar for Best Foreign Film. Pauline Kael, the great movie critic for *The New Yorker* magazine, gushed over it, saying "*Z* is almost intolerably exciting—a political thriller that builds up so much tension that you'll probably feel all knotted up by the time it's over." Most of all, though, she was impressed that the film worked, not just as political statement, but as a movie, and a commercial movie at that. It is a film that tells a great story and doesn't make viewers feel as though they are being forced to take their medicine. "*Z* is undoubtedly intended as a political act," Kael wrote, "but it never loses emotional contact with the audience."

The success of *Z* allowed Costa-Gavras a chance to work on a bigger stage, and through the 1970s his work continued to champion the victims of political oppression, in films most often starring a good friend of his, the masterly French actor Yves Montand. The director is probably best known in the United States for his 1982 film *Missing*, in which Jack Lemmon and Sissy Spacek play the father and wife of a young journalist who's captured while investigating the Pinochet regime in Chile. The two fight corporate power and diplomatic indifference in this story based on Thomas Hauser's book, which is in turn based on a journalist's true story. Again, Costa-Gavras had a major success on his hands, along with four Oscar nominations, including one for each of his lead actors. (He ended up with one win, for his adapted screenplay.)

The director's sense of outrage has barely diminished with age, though he continues to make films that are quite entertaining even as they question authority (and make their audiences do the same). In 2002, his film *Amen* took on another extremely tough subject: the charges that the Vatican turned a blind eye to the Nazi persecution of the Jews during World War II.

Nicholas Gage

Between 1940 and 1949, Greece was at war, not just with the Axis forces led by Nazi Germany but also within itself. A group of Communist rebels had attempted to seize power from the Greek government, leading to a series of ugly battles that amounted to civil war. Especially in the northern mountain regions of Greece, small bands of Communist guerrillas (funded by Yugoslavia, standing in for the Soviet Union) clashed with the forces of the Greek army (backed by the United States and Great Britain). One of those battles took place in 1948 in a tiny village called Lia, just below the Albanian border, where the guerrillas executed thirteen people and herded everyone else into refugee camps.

This would probably be a forgotten story of typical wartime brutality, except for a quirk of history and an iron will. One of the murdered villagers was a woman named Eleni Gatzoyiannis, who had taken a stand and refused to let the guerrillas conscript her children. Her only son, Nicholas, aged nine, was among the refugees taken over to Albania. Eventually, he was sent to the United States to live with his father, who had immigrated there years before and found a job in Massachusetts. Nicholas, like so many Greek Americans of his generation, was fiercely indoctrinated with the value of education. He made it through college and became a ferocious investigative journalist under the shortened by-line of Nicholas Gage.

The young reporter built his career at the *New York Times*, writing often about government misbehavior and organized crime. But his mother's story ate at him—"It was with me waking and sleeping," he later wrote—and he persuaded the *Times* to open an Athens bureau and then assign him there. Beginning from that base, he poured himself into work that was part journalistic investigation, part personal history, part detective work, and part pure revenge. Gage wanted to find the men who had sentenced his mother to death and the soldiers who had shot her and then confront them face-to-face.

He did, and the result was a monumental book titled *Eleni,* published in 1983. It is a unique piece of journalism because there is none of the detached observation typical of such a work. It is filled with fury, especially in several scenes where the author meets those involved with his mother's death and admits that he entertains thoughts of attacking them. Confronting one of the party of soldiers who shot his mother, he writes: "I had a quick image of smashing Taki's smiling face open on the marble table before us, but I sat there, forcing myself not to move as he talked on." In the climactic scene at the end of the book, he seeks out the judge who condemned his mother, and goes to the man's house armed with a tape recorder—and a Walther PPK pistol. (You'll need to read the book to find out what happens.) The utterly compelling story—as much about family bonds as about war and politics—was a best-seller in the U.S., and it occupies a space on a bookshelf in seemingly every Greek American home one visits.

Gage's career did not, of course, end with this success. His most recent book, *Greek Fire*, is a hugely entertaining dual biography of Aristotle Onassis and Maria Callas. Their stormy relationship was a basic food group to the gossip columnists of the 1950s and 1960s, and Gage's well-researched account of their difficulties was likewise a hit. He has also ventured into film, with both a successful adaptation of *Eleni*, starring John Malkovich and Kate Nelligan, and a role as executive producer of the third film in Francis Ford Coppola's *Godfather* trilogy. To this day, he lives in Worcester, Massachusetts, not far from where he settled with his father on his arrival in the United States.

Jeffrey Eugenides

It may not have been exactly a surprise when Jeffrey Eugenides' *Middlesex* won the Pulitzer Prize for Literature in 2003. The big, sprawling novel told the story of a Greek American immigrant family through several generations, and was ambitious in scope, successful in execution—all qualities that win awards for novels. Besides, the author had already achieved some attention with his previous book, *The Virgin Suicides*, and the successful movie drawn from it. But it certainly was an audacious subject for a novelist to attack, because the novel's family, originating in Smyrna and eventually settling in Detroit and its suburbs, has what can certainly be called a quirk: a history of intermarriage that leads up to the birth of Calliope, the narrator, who is a hermaphrodite. Born with a tangle of interrelated genetics, Calliope is (outwardly, at least) a girl in childhood, but starting at the age of about fourteen, she grows confused over her male and female characteristics and spends her adulthood as a man named Cal.

It's not the first time Eugenides has written uniquely about the differences between the sexes. His first novel, *The Virgin Suicides*, is about the Lisbon family, a household of five daughters in the affluent suburb of Grosse Pointe, Michigan. When one daughter kills herself, the results have cascading effects on the rest of the family. But the story's told as much through the eyes of several local boys, who idolize the Lisbon girls, as through the girls themselves, and the author often seems to be examining the way men view women. (Not incidentally, Eugenides' first novel became an extremely well-regarded first film directed by the young Sofia Coppola.)

Middlesex, aside from being a book about sexual complexity, is a lovely memoir of growing up Greek in the American Midwest. Various members of the family are in the diner and bar businesses (as well as some shadier ventures); they work terribly hard by day and play rebetiko records at night. They revel in their American success, buying homes and cars that are a little flashy and off-key by the standards of well-bred America—especially a big house called "Middlesex" that is full of weird architectural features. Meanwhile, of course, the sprawl of American culture from 1922 to the late 1970s (where the book's action begins and ends) is there in all its complexity: the Depression, the war, race riots, urban decay, affluence, drugs. Even the Nation of Islam makes an appearance.

All good novels draw to some extent on the author's own life and upbringing, and Eugenides's are no exception. Certainly, the Michigan settings of his books reflect his own upbringing there; moreover, how could a writer who saw the Detroit riots of the 1960s not someday want to talk about them? In an interview with fellow novelist Jonathan Safran Foer just before the book's release, Eugenides explained how a family memoir fit into a book about such a strange topic: "At first I just wanted to write a fictional memoir of a hermaphrodite. This summoned other literary hermaphrodites, like Tiresias. Hermaphroditism led to classicism. Classicism led to Hellenism. And Hellenism led to my family. I used my Greek ancestry because it worked in the story I wanted to tell, not the other way around. But with a name like Eugenides, what do you expect?"

Nana Mouskouri

Let's start with the eyeglasses. In the late 1950s, when Nana Mouskouri appeared on the international music scene, women performers didn't wear glasses—it was either contact lenses or squinting. Yet here was this young Greek woman with not only eyeglasses but big clunky ones. Maybe it was inevitable that they'd become not a joke but a distinctive visual signature, one that distinguished her from the pack and that fans still remember to this day.

Of course, the glasses are hardly the source of Mouskouri's mystique. That honor goes to her voice, trained from her earliest years. Born in Crete in 1934, Joanna Mouskouri was nicknamed Nana as a small girl. Nana grew up in a house full of music (her mother a singer as well, her father a movie projectionist), and her parents knew early on that their daughter had an especially worthy voice. Her Athens music teacher is said to have continued teaching her for free when her parents could not afford lessons, lest her talent go to waste. Eventually, she made it to the Athens Conservatory of Music, where she defied the professors who insisted that she sing only classical work, and began to perform popular and jazz tunes in the city's clubs. An early professional relationship with the musician Manos Hadjidakis helped her find her idiom, and she befriended the composer Iannis Xenakis and the actor Melina Mercouri, who gave her further professional guidance.

A mounting reputation in Greece expanded to the rest of Europe. There Mouskouri began to build a real following, especially in France, where she would settle and have her greatest success. (She eventually learned to sing in French.) She also met up with the record producer Quincy Jones, who in 1962 recorded her for an American release titled *The Girl from Greece Sings*. It provided her first big hit single, a song called "The White Rose of Athens," and the album sold over a million copies. Possibly her best-known American record, a duet with Harry Belafonte called *An Evening with Belafonte / Mouskouri,* was released the next year, to considerable commercial and critical response.

Since those early successes, her career has been, to put it simply, unprecedented. Over more than forty years, she's recorded more than one thousand songs in ten languages. Bob Dylan is a huge fan, and he even wrote a song expressly for her after hearing her sing in concert. One of her most celebrated moments came in 1984, when she performed in the Herod Atticus Theater at the base of the Acropolis. It was the first time she'd performed in Greece in more than twenty years, and she received huge acclaim at home, especially after the concert was broadcast and released on disc. (Since then, she's returned for encore performances.)

She's also broadened her interests to include politics, serving in the European parliament and as an ambassador for UNICEF. In her long career, she's sold an incredible 200 million records—and counting, for Nana Mouskouri continues to tour and record regularly. And to this day, she's never stopped wearing those big black clunky eyeglasses.

Telly Savalas

For a few years in the 1970s, it was the television catchphrase that was on every high-schooler's lips, a casual, swingin' greeting with just a hint of a leer: *Who loves ya, baby?* Moreover, nobody needed to explain where it came from. Everybody knew that it was the pet phrase of a shaven-headed, lollipop-sucking, crime-fighting TV cop by the name of Lieutenant Theo Kojak—the signature role that branded the smiling face of Telly Savalas into a small but memorable bit of TV history. Not incidentally, the character, a major ladies' man, also became a hero to bald men everywhere.

Savalas—the Telly is short for Aristotle, by the way—will forever be best known as Kojak, but it was hardly his only big role. He'd broken into acting when Burt Lancaster spotted him, and he broke into the public eye with an appearance alongside his mentor in the film *Birdman of Alcatraz*, a role for which he received an Oscar nomination for Best Supporting Actor. High-profile roles—traditionally difficult for an actor with strong features and an "ethnic" look—followed, most memorably in *Genghis Khan*, the James Bond film *On Her Majesty's Secret Service* (where he played the great Bond villain Ernst Stavro Blofeld), and as Pontius Pilate in the Bible epic *The Greatest Story Ever Told*.

That epic film is significant for one other piece of Savalasiana: it is the one where the director, George Stevens, suggested that if Savalas shaved his head it would make him look more powerful and virile. It turned out that he was right, of course, and his star retained the look for the rest of his life, even amid thousands of jokes about bowling balls and chrome domes. Soon after, he was cast in a TV movie titled *The Marcus-Nelson Murders*, as a New York City police detective with a faintly Greek name. The show was a hit; CBS thought Savalas's character had potential and spun off the series that would last for five successful seasons (and would costar his brother, George Savalas, who appeared in the credits under his Greek name, Demetrios).

Savalas's memorable look may have been one reason for *Kojak's* success, but it's hardly the only one. A lot of the appeal of the show came from the actor's charm and ease on camera. His character, an outsider figure who tended to look askance at rules, drew heavily on his own charisma, and audiences responded. His characteristic quirks were also memorable—especially those lollipops he constantly kept in his mouth, a habit that Savalas revealed in interviews he'd adopted to quit smoking, in part because he didn't want to be a bad influence on young viewers. He even brought his background into the show, dropping Greek ad-libs into the scripted lines.

Once *Kojak* made him famous and well-off, Savalas could work if he wished and took smaller movie parts (including one in *The Muppet Movie*, as a character with the fabulous name El Sleezo Tough). He also stuck with his best-known role, revisiting it in several TV movies in the decade after the series went off the air in 1978. His financial freedom allowed him to indulge in a serious card-playing habit, and he even made an instructional film about how to win at blackjack. Unfortunately, his post-*Kojak* career was not as long as his fans had wished: Savalas died one day after his seventieth birthday in 1994, shortly after a big party with his family.

John Cassavetes

Plenty of movie actors say "what I really want to do is direct," so much so that the line has become an interview cliché. But few make it to the other side of the camera in any meaningful way. Woody Allen is an exception, though one might argue that he is hardly an actor, as he plays characters that vary so little from film to film. Martin Scorsese pops up on-screen regularly, though usually in his own films and in bit parts. But not many filmmakers have managed to exist comfortably in both worlds, except John Cassavetes. He is the rakish bad-boy actor who became one of the great avant-garde directors of the 1960s.

Born to Greek-immigrant parents on Long Island, Cassavetes began his career like a lot of actors, with a degree from the New York Academy of Dramatic Arts (in 1950) and small parts in movies over the next few years, which got him typecast as a "troubled youth" in the manner of Marlon Brando or James Dean. (He also married the young actress Gena Rowlands, with whom he'd stay for the rest of his life.) But he quickly became more interested in the filmmaking process and, in 1956, began trying to turn an idea from an acting class he'd taught into a feature film. (He'd a uniquely aggressive method of obtaining funds: he mentioned the idea during an appearance on Jean Shepherd's popular radio show and asked listeners to send in checks. Cassavetes received $20,000, enough to pique the interests of larger investors and get the project off the ground.) The film, titled *Shadows*, would take him two years to complete and was a milestone in fifties cinema, bringing together highly realistic dialogue, handheld camera work, and the improvisational quality of the Beat generation's writing. It was controversial, dealing with the then troublesome subject of interracial marriage. And it was a success, especially in Europe; it's often cited today as an early exponent of the emerging style called cinema verité and is also remembered for its score by the great jazz bassist Charles Mingus.

The studios noticed, and Paramount signed Cassavetes to a deal—which lasted one film. *Too Late Blues*, about a jazz musician torn between making unthreatening music that will bring him popular success and the inventive work that feeds his soul, was a box-office dud. In a turn of events that mirrored the film's story, Paramount dropped him. His *A Child Is Waiting*, released the next year, caused him even more career headaches: Cassavetes was working for the bigwig producer Stanley Kramer, who disliked the director's final edit and fired him, choosing to recut the film himself and give it a more sentimental tone. Cassavetes was publicly critical of the result, and Hollywood noticed that as well. Always a fiery character, he'd acquired an unfortunate new reputation as a "difficult" director.

If he wanted to make films from here on out, Cassavetes knew that he'd have to raise the money himself. So he returned to acting, including a few performances for which he's quite fondly remembered. In *The Dirty Dozen*, he plays a murderer retrained and sent off to attack the Nazis. And in Roman Polanski's *Rosemary's Baby*, he plays Rosemary's actor husband, Guy Woodhouse, who—well, if you've seen it, you remember what he does, and if you haven't, we won't spoil the ending here. (Suffice it to say that he's not exactly an ideal dad.) Cassavetes even appeared alongside Ronald Reagan, then in the final years of his acting career, in a gangster flick called *The Killers*.

The income from these jobs paid for Cassavetes' next film, and quite a film it was. *Faces,* released in 1968 and starring Gena Rowlands, is a tense psychological portrait of a rotting marriage. It took the director six months to shoot and years to edit (his first cut was six hours long). Rich in emotional texture and very slow moving, the film is, for many viewers, difficult to watch. Cassavetes himself explained why he was less interested in action than in his characters' inner life: "I've never seen an exploding helicopter, I've never seen anybody go and blow somebody's head off. So why should I make films about them? But I have seen people destroy themselves in the smallest possible way. I've seen people withdraw. I've seen people hide behind political ideas, behind dope, behind the sexual revolution, behind fascism, behind hypocrisy." The result is a high-water mark for sixties films, and an inspiration to indie filmmakers since then.

His experience with *Faces* defined the rest of Cassavetes' career:

regular work on Hollywood projects would bring in enough cash to fund his own art films. His 1970 *Husbands*, starring Peter Falk and Ben Gazzara along with Cassavetes himself, examines three suburban guys who discover new things about themselves after a friend's death. He reached a high point in 1974 with *A Woman Under the Influence*, starring Rowlands and Falk as a married couple dealing with the wife's mental illness. Many say it's the director's greatest film, and it even achieved a certain amount of mainstream success, including Oscar nominations for the director and star. Unfortunately, his career after that was relatively brief, only about a decade; in 1989, just as the independent-film movement he'd helped create was entering its boom years, Cassavetes died from liver disease brought on by many years of alcoholism. In his memory, the Independent Film Project—the largest association of moviemakers who work outside the studio system—gives out an award named for Cassavetes each year. It's presented to the best film made for under $500,000.

Nia Vardalos

In the mid-1990s, Nia Vardalos, a comedian and actor living in Los Angeles, California, had spun a bunch of droll stories about her Greek American relatives into a one-woman show. As she tells the story, she had enough money for a short run and for one advertisement—a tiny one-day ad in the *Los Angeles Times*. Ordinarily, such a show plays for a couple of weeks to friends of the performer and a smattering of other theatergoers—except that in this case, the ad caught the eye of Rita Wilson, the Greek American actor who is married to Tom Hanks. Wilson showed up at the theater, liked the show, and told her husband it was movie material; they tracked down Vardalos and offered to produce it as a film.

Since Vardalos insisted that she, instead of an established star, would have to play the lead, the producers made the film on a modest budget without studio backing. But something mysterious happened in 2002, when *My Big Fat Greek Wedding* landed in theaters. This playful small film struck a nerve with moviegoers of every ethnicity. A long, slow build followed as word of mouth led to its release on more and more screens, in more and more cities. Within a few months, the little film had become—as headline writers across the country delighted in telling readers—a Big Fat Greek Success. The final tally, in just the United States, was well over $200 million, for a movie that cost less than $5 million to make.

How did it happen? It was partly being in the right place at the right time. Recent seasons had been short on films meant for female moviegoers, and they flocked to see Vardalos's film. But more than that, *My Big Fat Greek Wedding* hit notes familiar to every American with an extended ethnic family, no matter what its derivation. Greek or not, everyone has a crazy aunt, a dopey cousin or two, or a parent who gripes about how her children aren't married off yet, and the experiences were familiar yet fresh to non-Greek audiences, who came back over and over. On top of that, Vardalos has a knack for characters—especially the father, played by Michael Constantine. In what may be the script's most memorable quirk, Constantine's character has persuaded himself that Windex is some kind of cure-all, and throughout the movie, he's spraying it on people, soaking their elbows in it, and generally spritzing it everywhere. It's a bit of scriptwriting that's just odd enough to take an audience by surprise while evoking something very familiar (don't *your* elderly relatives have a few strange ideas?), and Vardalos's eye for such detail is what made audiences so responsive.

So responsive, in fact, that Vardalos took the film to TV. In early 2003, CBS premiered a situation comedy based on her characters called

My Big Fat Greek Life. Vardalos starred, and nearly all the film's actors came with her. Unfortunately, she couldn't replicate the film's jokey interactions on the small screen. Where the humor in the film had been based on long scenes and subplots, the setup-punchline-setup-punchline rhythm of TV didn't treat the characters kindly. Vardalos looked stiff and ill at ease. Furthermore, stories began to leak out that her sudden success had gone to her head and that she'd become combative and demanding, a diva on the set. Whatever the reason, the show started huge in the ratings—no surprise, given that the film had effectively advertised it for a year—and faded almost immediately. The series was canceled after barely two months. Her next film, *Connie and Carla*, was also a commercial disappointment. Still, Vardalos is likely to land on her feet. She's learned to negotiate the Hollywood system, and given the success of her movie, she has a big fat bankroll for future projects.

Vangelis

It's so familiar that it's become a punch line, an automatic cue for laughter: the scene in any film when an athlete approaches peak performance and the director cuts to slow motion. You can almost bet that the soundtrack will begin with an echoing electronic beat that rises and falls, followed by a piano riff that every moviegoer on the planet can recognize. Somewhere right now, in some theater or screening room, someone is crossing a finish line, arms raised, or driving toward a basketball hoop, and the music underneath is the theme music from *Chariots of Fire*.

The composer Vangelis—born Evangelos O. Papathanassiou—is, of course, best known for his *Chariots* soundtrack, which won him an Academy Award in 1982. But it's far from his only successful work. In Greece in the 1960s, he was an early exponent of electronic pop, filling stadiums with fans who came to hear his band Formynx. At the time of the coup in 1968, he left Greece and moved to Paris, where he began working on film scores, especially with the French director Frédéric

Rossif. After flirting with an offer to join the progressive rock band Yes in the early 1970s, he declined after a few weeks' rehearsals, saying they and he didn't make the same kind of music. Gradually, he moved into film work full time, and soon cooked up the theme that would be his signature (and one of the most successful such recordings ever). Most of his films have been European productions, unfamiliar to American audiences. But recently he took on a project that would get much larger attention in the United States. Oliver Stone's *Alexander*, the epic screen biography of the Macedonian general Alexander the Great who ruled nearly the entire known world, starred Colin Farrell and Angelina Jolie, and was expected to be a substantial blockbuster in late 2004; Greeks and Macedonians got into yet another series of arguments over Alexander's legacy and the depiction of his homosexuality in the film. (For multiple reasons, the film ended up a box-office stinker.) The advance word suggesting that the film's Alexander would reach Persia on foot, bursting through finish-line tape in slow motion, turned out to be false.

Yanni

All right, we'll get it out in the open. A lot of people think Yanni is funny, and it's not exactly clear why. Is it his soft-edged music, which is tough to characterize but usually gets tossed into the New Age bin at the record store? Is it the name, which sounds sort of goofy as it rolls off American tongues? Is it that his fans tend toward the crystal-wearing and mellow rather than the urban and hip? (If you ask me, it's the hair, that fluffy black mane that looks like he blow-dries it twice a day. Beaded with sweat, it catches the light just so onstage, and it photographs very, very well indeed.)

Doesn't matter. Yanni—formerly Yiannis Chryssomallis—is the defining figure of New Age music. Being the most successful in any idiom, whether critics roll their eyes or not, is a really big deal, and he's the biggest New Age performer ever, the Elvis Presley of his genre. The self-taught pianist sold more than 7 million copies of his 1994 album *Yanni Live at the Acropolis*, the companion film of which is still a pledge-week staple on PBS stations all over America. (And apparently people can't watch it often enough: although it airs regularly, he's sold 750,000 copies of it on video too.) His more recent televised concerts, from places as diverse as the Royal Albert Hall in London and the Forbidden City in Beijing, have been similar successes. He performed the national anthem at one game of the 2003 World Series. His autobiography, *Yanni in Words*, published in 2002, made it onto the best-seller lists. He's even been involved in a high-profile relationship, which kept him in the tabloids for years, with the TV actor Linda Evans.

Moreover, even if you don't go for his music—and if he's selling that many albums, a whole lot of people are buying them without admitting to it—you have to admit that he's a man who's totally devoted to his craft. After coming to America for college in 1972, he started a band called Chameleon and worked in obscurity for more than a decade until tracks from his first albums started to pop up on the radio in the mid-1980s. From then on, he devoted himself to his music almost monastically—touring, promoting, and recording constantly.

He's worked on his music, as he puts it, "sixteen hours a day in a room, for twenty years." Furthermore, Yanni and his team of producers concocted a singularly visual kind of concert: the megaperformance in an exotic locale. He sets up a stage somewhere utterly recognizable, like the Taj Mahal, and flies in equipment, lighting, smoke machines, and about a million orchestral musicians in tuxedoes. It's all about spectacle and wrapping the audience in the moment, and it's incredibly popular, to the point where he's spawned a minimovement of imitators, like John Tesh. (Tesh, in particular, could be called Son of Yanni—especially because he began his career touring with the master.) Yanni has ridden that formula to one of the biggest music careers in the world, one that—in part because he doesn't sing and, therefore, faces no language barrier—has made him a star all over the planet. Still laughing? So is he.

Elia Kazan

As a filmmaker, Elia Kazan was without equal. He was often called the greatest "actors' director" ever, the man who got superb performances out of such screen icons as James Dean, Natalie Wood, and especially the young and erratic Marlon Brando. But when Kazan stepped up to receive his lifetime-achievement Academy Award in 1999—usually among the warmest moments in a moviemaker's career—the applause was far from wholehearted, as some members of the Academy sat on their hands and protesters shouted outside the auditorium. In the early 1950s, when Congress was investigating former members of the Communist Party, Kazan, a former member of the movement, was called to testify. Faced with a choice between professional suicide and turning in his old friends and colleagues, he chose the latter, a decision that would follow him forever.

In terms of his art, Elia Kazan (family name: Kazanjoglous) really can't be faulted. His career began on the stage, and he'd return to Broadway quite regularly during his life. On-screen, he broke through into the public eye with *A Tree Grows in Brooklyn* in 1945, following it up with *Gentleman's Agreement*, an indictment of anti-Semitism starring Gregory Peck that got him his first Oscar. *A Streetcar Named Desire*, his majestic filmed version of the Tennessee Williams play, introduced Brando to the world. (You doubtless remember him in his torn T-shirt, yelling "Stella!") The gorgeously shot tale about a sadly wrecked New Orleans household is one of the few films adapted from a theatrical play that really does the original justice.

It was in the spring of 1952, not long after the release of *Streetcar*, when Kazan's political life heated up. A few years earlier, a Congressional group called the House Un-American Activities Committee (HUAC) had begun investigations meant to find Communists in Hollywood, especially those who had joined the Communist Party two decades earlier, when it was at its peak of popularity and membership. Movie stars such as Humphrey Bogart were called; so were screenwriters such as Dalton Trumbo and Ring Lardner, Jr. Ultimately, ten of them (known as the Hollywood Ten) would refuse to name names, and none of them would work regularly, except under pseudonyms, for at least a decade. Their careers were ruined. The investigation continued into the 1950s, and when Kazan was called before Congress, he was unsure of what to do. He didn't want to sell out his friends; he also didn't want his career destroyed for protecting a group whose beliefs he had vigorously rejected. (By this time, Kazan had become an anti-Communist.) After talking the situation over with colleagues—and under severe pressure from the heads of Twentieth Century-Fox—Kazan decided to tell the committee what he knew. He named names.

The backlash started almost instantly. His colleagues denounced and shunned Kazan, especially old friends like the writer Lillian Hellman. Some prominent actors said they would never work for him, including Marlon Brando, who quickly recanted his decision when he realized that Kazan had been his most effective director. The two would come together for one more project, and it was a big one. *On the Waterfront*, released in 1954, was probably Kazan's greatest film and Brando's greatest success up to that time. The story of corruption and brutality among New Jersey longshoremen was a smash both critically and financially. Many viewers also saw it as a veiled allegory for, and justification of, Kazan's political actions.

Ironically, Kazan's career, which he'd hoped to save by cooperating with Congress, ended up damaged anyway. Producers and studios declared him "too controversial," making it difficult for him to find work for some time. Though he made several more significant films, especially *Splendor in the Grass*, starring Natalie Wood, he worked less and less throughout the sixties. His final film was *The Last Tycoon*, in 1976, though he'd live another quarter of a century, dying at ninety-three in 2003.

Greg Louganis

Diving is one of those sports that few Americans follow. Until it pops up in the Olympics every four years, enthusiasts are generally the only ones paying attention. But at the 1984 Olympic Games in Los Angeles, California, one diver did become a household name—the only one in living memory, really—and by dint of his good looks and charisma, Greg Louganis has stayed in the public eye ever since. He is, simply, the greatest diver ever.

To start with, he was a prodigy: he'd won an Olympic medal (a silver, in 1976) at the breathtaking age of sixteen. By the 1984 games, he was preeminent in his sport and was the first man in half a century to take home the gold in both platform and springboard diving events. Four years later, during the preliminary dives at the Seoul Olympics—at a point when he was beginning to be considered too old for competition—he had a close call that almost kept him out of the games, hitting his head on the tip of the board during a dive. Louganis came away with a nasty gash on his head, and had it sutured up quickly so that he could return and finish his dives half an hour later. Not only did he qualify, but a few days later, he won the double gold for the second time and did it with a reverse three-and-a-half somersault that had been nicknamed the Dive of Death, after the two athletes who'd been killed trying it.

Louganis at that time was at the pinnacle of his athletic career. But he revealed years later, he was also a very unhappy person who was living with a secret: he was a gay man, one who, like many athletes afraid of locker-room retribution, had kept his sexuality quiet. A few months before the Games, he'd discovered that he'd been infected with HIV, the virus that causes AIDS. Louganis had in fact expected to drop out of the competition, but his doctors told him that he'd be able to compete, and he decided to press onward to what would become his greatest success. But because he hadn't announced his illness, the doctors who sutured him up at the Olympics didn't know to take particular pains to avoid infection themselves—a situation that once he revealed his HIV status caused a mild controversy, though everyone involved turned out to be fine.

Over the next several years, as his fame crested, Louganis debated whether to reveal his sexual preference to the world. Ultimately—and, he admits, with lots of help from family, friends, and a therapist—he came out of the closet publicly at the Gay Games in 1994, before what he wryly calls "a pretty supportive crowd." A year later, in an interview with Barbara Walters, he admitted to his HIV-positive status. He's also managed to build a second career, avoiding the somewhat forlorn life that many Olympians encounter after their competitive years end.

Louganis has provided color commentary during televised diving competitions and, helped by his easy charm, has even dabbled in acting, receiving notice for several modest parts on the New York stage and in the movies. He's also active as a spokesperson for gay issues and AIDS charities, and his autobiography, *Breaking the Surface*, spent several weeks at the top of the best-seller lists in 1995.

Constantine Cavafy

His name may be a bit less well known than that of T. S. Eliot or W. H. Auden, but those great poets considered Constantine Cavafy at least their equal. Born in Alexandria, Egypt—then under the influence of the Turks—to ethnic Greek parents in 1863, Cavafy moved to England as a child and then back to Egypt as a teenager. As a young man, he completely embraced the classics, cultivating a passion for ancient Greek literature and history so deep that as soon as he was old enough he became a Greek citizen. Several years spent living in Constantinople's Greek district only deepened his national pride and also got him thinking about the two versions of modern Greek—the demotic, or populist spoken language, and the purist form called *kathevarousa*—and about how they mixed together. Those two interests would define much of his work to come.

Although his family encouraged his writing and his brother, especially, lent him some financial support, Cavafy, like many poets, had to hold down a day job. In his case, that meant a clerkship in Alexandria's

Ministry of Irrigation. (The records there show that his bosses found him very valuable, not least because he spoke six or so languages.) He also worked as a broker on Alexandria's stock exchange, all the while writing poems, during his evenings and other free time, in his book-filled apartment on Lepsius Street and in the city's cafés.

Cavafy was reluctant to publish, especially in his early career, when he was troubled by self-doubt. He would send his poetry to many friends for review but destroyed the vast majority of his work, keeping only what he considered the very best. During his lifetime, he published only two books, the first when he was forty-one, although by the time of his death his fame had begun to grow and he did have a devoted circle of admirers in Alexandria and in the Hellenic world. E. M. Forster, the British author who wrote so eloquently about Alexandria after being stationed there during World War I, also became a good friend and introduced Cavafy's work to Eliot and other literary figures. Though Cavafy was homosexual and openly so—many of the poems are quite frank on the subject—the taboos of the day did not seem to hurt his popularity very much.

As with so many literary figures, Cavafy found his widest fame posthumously. Two years after his death in 1933, his collected poems were published in a single volume and eventually translated into many languages. (Later editions include a lovely appreciation by Auden.) They reveal to modern ears a richness of education, especially: Cavafy writes from the point of view of ancient heroes and mythical figures and from places all over the Hellenic world. His best-known poem,

"Ithaca," has a simple beauty that shines through even in translation (here by Rae Dalven) and speaks of universal truths but also of the poet's journey of discovery itself:

When you start on your journey to Ithaca,
then pray that the road is long,
full of adventure, full of knowledge. . . .
And if you find her poor, Ithaca has not defrauded you.
With the great wisdom you have gained, with so much experience,
you must surely have understood by then what Ithaca means.

Odysseus Elytis

The poetic invention of Odysseus Elytis extends even to his name. Though his parents supplied the "Odysseus"—and how could he end up anything but a poet, with a name straight out of Homer?—the writer himself created his surname, a loose compound of the Greek words *Hellas* (Greece), *elpidha* (hope), *eleftheria* (freedom), and *Eleni* (Helen). It's a sort of poetic manifesto, suggesting a reach for linguistic invention, lofty ideas, and beauty.

Elytis's works live out that manifesto. Like many Modern Greek poets, he reached back for ancient themes. Unlike many, however, he used them only as jumping-off points, focusing his writing on the contemporary world and the eternal Greece: the wind, the light, the sea. His later works grow darker, touching on subjects like grief and the search for a final paradise. His best-known book, *The Axion Esti* ("It Is Worthy"), is a three-part hymn to Greece itself, told through the persona of a narrator who gradually becomes the voice of his country. Its three parts are all told through the lens of Christianity and Hellenism together: the first part establishes the creation of the narrator and his consciousness of the world, the second part tells of his horrific wartime experience, and the third celebrates the vitality of the world despite all that he's seen. The poem is often compared to Walt Whitman's "Song of Myself."

Much of what we read in *The Axion Esti* is, of course, drawn from Elytis's own life. Born in Crete in 1911—his original surname was Alepoudhelis—he himself served in combat during World War II. During the Greek civil war that followed, he left Greece, settling in Paris and coming to know that city's avant-garde intellectual circle, falling in with the likes of Picasso and Breton. In subsequent years, when he returned to Greece, he wrote, published, and helped run seemingly every cultural institution in the country, from the Greek National Radio Foundation to the National Theatre.

Unlike many in the European avant-garde, however, Elytis had a populist touch. His works (in Greek and in translation) remain a favorite among young students who read poetry, a bit like Whitman's are in the United States. His popularity was helped as well by a lovely musical setting of *The Axion Esti* composed by Mikis Theodorakis. Elytis worked in other idioms as well—creating collages, translating other poets, and composing essays about his poetic ideas for publication. And in 1979, his body of work received the highest honor given to literary figures: a call from Sweden told Elytis that he had received the Nobel Prize in Literature. The formal presentation cited "his poetry, which, against the background of Greek tradition, depicts with sensuous strength and intellectual clear-sightedness modern man's struggle for freedom and creativeness." It is worthy indeed.

Dean Tavoularis

What exactly does a film's production designer do? He or she isn't a costume or set designer, a hairstylist, or a prop builder, yet all those things are major parts of his or her job. The production designer's job is to unify and manage every visual aspect of the film. A director will decide, for example, that "this film is set in 1940," and it's the production designer's task to convey 1940 through everything from the color of the lighting to finding period props to helping decide on camera angles that make the film look right. At its best, it creates a film-going experience that envelops an audience, building a mood and atmosphere that reinforces the actors' work without calling attention to itself. It's one of those jobs that's hard to see when it's done well.

Which is why you may not know the name Dean Tavoularis. But Tavoularis is one of the great production designers in Hollywood, with a pile of Oscar nominations and an extraordinary list of credits attached to his name. His career began as an art director, most prominently on *Bonnie and Clyde* in 1967, but it was really when he began collaborating with the director Francis Ford Coppola that he started to achieve something special. Their first work together was *The Godfather*, declared by many critics to be the greatest American film ever made. Working on a surprisingly tight budget—at least for the first installment of what would become a trilogy—Tavoularis transformed the Lower East Side of New York into its thirty-years-earlier self. (He'd had to lobby for real sets: the studio wanted to save money by using a fake New York on its back lot.) Along with the cinematographer Gordon Willis, they created a visual palette, aided by new techniques of overhead lighting, that added age and mystery. In fact, the DVD release of the *Godfather* films includes a tour by Tavoularis, laying out in detail how he reworked New York streets for the film.

The first two *Godfather* films established a professional relationship between Coppola and Tavoularis, and the two continue to work together to this day. Coppola's *Apocalypse Now*, made in 1979, is remembered as one of the most disastrous location shoots ever, crashing into nearly endless obstacles, from typhoons to star Martin Sheen's heart attack. Through it all, the director came out with a masterpiece, greatly aided by the murky visual style built by Tavoularis. The jungle encampment of Colonel Kurtz, based loosely on the Cambodian temples at Angkor Wat, is often singled out for praise.

Nor has their collaboration stopped there. More recent films, such as the underrated *Tucker*, continue to be striking pieces of production design, and Tavoularis even contributed his skills to *CQ*, the debut film by Coppola's son Roman. Another long-term collaboration, a science fiction film set in New York called *Megalopolis*, should be on screens in 2006 or so. No matter whether that project is successful, however, Tavoularis's reputation is unassailable. Younger designers idolize him—Stuart Craig, who did the *Harry Potter* films, is a particular admirer—and the films speak for themselves.

George Lois

The first sentence of George Lois's autobiography, *George, Be Careful*, catches you like a bear trap: "When I was a kid and an Irishman croaked, I worked my balls off." Never mind, for the moment, what it means (for the record, Lois grew up as the son of a florist in an Irish neighborhood in the Bronx, and the delivery orders would overwhelm the shop when a big funeral came around). The point is that it's distilled, incredibly eye-catching language, the kind of sentence you can't ignore, even if you're a little put off by the crass turn of phrase. You start there, and there is *no* chance you'll put that book down.

Lois has constructed a career out of moves like that, and it's made him one of the most revered figures in the advertising world. Starting at the premier creative firm of the late 1950s, Doyle Dane Bernbach, and at his own agencies later on, Lois helped pioneer a vast change in the advertising world, from patient explanations of a product's virtue—the kind of thing that would work only in a quiet world where readers weren't constantly assaulted with messages—to the punchy, funny, vigorous kind of advertising we know today. ("Advertising is poison gas," Lois once said. "It should absolutely attack you; it should rip your lungs out!") Even forty years on, many of Lois's early ads are still effective at slinging a slogan. (Mickey Mantle cried "I want my Maypo!" for Lois, and the Braniff slogan "If you got it, flaunt it" worked its way into the larger culture, to the point where few people even think of it as a tagline anymore.)

If his ads have big personalities, Lois has a bigger one. A street tough from the Bronx, he is famous for his temper, his impossibly high-energy pitches to clients, and his take-no-prisoners approach to the office soft-ball league. And nowhere did that personality come through as on his magazine covers. In the early 1960s, the editor of *Esquire*, a witty, canny southern gent named Harold Hayes, decided that his covers needed perking up and that a smart adman might be able to help. He called on Lois, offering him almost free rein, and their collaboration would be like no other in the magazine world—brilliant, controversial, and even commercially successful, as *Esquire*'s sales boomed. For a cover story about Muhammad Ali's trials, Lois did him up like St. Sebastian, bound and bristling with arrows. Lois put Lieutenant William Calley, who was on trial for the My Lai massacre in Vietnam, on the cover, grinning and surrounded by a group of Vietnamese children. (Lois explained the idea to his boss thus: "Those who think he's innocent will say that proves it. Those who think he's guilty will say that proves it.") And he showed Andy Warhol drowning in a can of Campbell's tomato soup, under the words "The final decline and total collapse of the American avant-garde," on a 1969 issue that editors often cite as one of the greatest magazine covers ever.

When his *Esquire* years ended (after Hayes was fired, having stirred up perhaps a little *too* much controversy), Lois returned to ads full time, producing campaigns for *USA Today*, *Time* magazine, Lean Cuisine—he cooked up that product's name, in fact—and many other companies, most quite successful. His most famous job came in the early 1980s, when a new channel was beginning to make its way onto cable TV. Local cable carriers were slow to add it to their systems, and Lois knew that this network, pitched to teenagers, was never going to get traction until the kids demanded it. So he gave them the words with which to call their cable companies, drawing on his old Maypo campaign. "I want my MTV!" was born, and nobody who was a teenager in 1982 doesn't remember those ads. Which may be why his retrospective collection *$ellebrity*, published in 2001, was another hot seller.

John and Jennifer Aniston

It was a momentous turn of events , at least for soap opera-fanatics. In February 2004, a *Days of Our Lives* character named Victor Kiriakis was killed off, electrocuted when a rival dropped a CD player into his bathtub. John Aniston had been playing the scheming, devious Kiriakis since 1985, hanging on for nearly two decades before receiving his highly dramatic death—the fate eventually meted out to nearly every daytime-drama star. (Then again, soap-opera deaths are highly situational. If the show needs an evil character, perhaps he'll turn out not to have been killed after all, or he'll have *a secret twin!*)

John Aniston himself has had many lives. Born in Crete, he came to the United States as a young man—the family name was Anistonopoulos, which he shortened for his credits—and began his career as a New York stage actor in musicals and dramas. He's also done film and prime-time TV, including guest shots on *Kojak* alongside his close friend Telly Savalas. But his real success was on daytime TV, where he's barely had a year off since the mid-1970s, starting with a now-defunct soap opera called *Love of Life.* He's also kept his hand in stage work, coming full circle recently with a successful run in a California production of Arthur Miller's *Death of a Salesman.*

As his *Days of Our Lives* character was zapped into oblivion, John wasn't the only Aniston drawing to the end of a long NBC run. As anyone with a TV set knew in May 2004, the sitcom *Friends*—certainly the network's most popular show and one of its hottest properties ever—was wrapping up amid a circus of hype. And although it's an ensemble show, with six actors billed alphabetically, the one who built the biggest career through the series was Jennifer Aniston, John's daughter. Despite playing a faintly unlikable role—her Rachel Green was a little needy, a little spoiled, a little self-absorbed—audiences adored the character and completely embraced Jennifer. (Not to mention her haircut, which turned into a national craze during the early years of the show.)

The younger Aniston might have had a slightly easier introduction to the acting world because of her dad's career. (Savalas was her godfather, in fact.) But she certainly paid her dues as well, in forgettable movies (*Leprechaun*, anyone?) and small sitcom gigs. Then came the monster hit that was *Friends*; since then, she has been on the A-list for romantic comedies and other big-screen work. She also drew attention to her range with the release in 2002 of *The Good Girl*, where she played a young, unhappily married woman working in a Texas discount store.

They're a Greek family, to be sure—when Jennifer was young, they'd go back to Crete for long stretches—but she's admitted in interviews that she's pretty much an all-American girl and has no patience with Greek households where "women are still second-class citizens, pregnant in the kitchen, while the men sit around drinking ouzo and smoking cigarettes after dinner instead of helping with anything. My dad is a Greek man and I love him with all my heart, but . . . Greek men are all about big moustaches, lots of ouzo and dancing with women who aren't necessarily their wives. And also their moms tell them they're perfect so they think they can do no wrong." No wonder she ended up with Brad Pitt, whom she married in 2000, long before he even flirted with Greek godhood in *Troy*. Their wedding in 2000 was the tabloid event of the year. And, unfortunately, so was their separation in 2005.

Olympia Dukakis

To hear Olympia Dukakis tell it, her career in the theater started early and inauspiciously. As a small child, Dukakis was recruited by her parents to play "the spirit of young Greece" onstage. The role involved releasing a cage of white doves, meant to fly over the audience at the climax of the play; the birds proceeded to do what birds do, right on the heads of the audience.

Fortunately for her career, Olympia Dukakis didn't quit the business, although she came close. Even though she'd been interested in theater in college, Dukakis didn't get onto the screen until she was well into her thirties. (She'd begun her adult life as a physical therapist—practical and decent-paying, she explained later.) Steady work in small roles followed; a look at her résumé reveals a staggering number of jobs credited as "John's mother," "Joey's mom," and so forth. Her strong features got her character parts too—middle-aged Greek ladies, Italian ladies, Polish ladies. She made a steady living playing the next-door neighbor who gets five minutes of "wisecracky" screen time. (Her husband, Louis Zorich, built a similar career on father-in-law roles.)

But a surprise lay in wait for her. In 1987, she took on a supporting role—as another Italian mom—in a romantic comedy about a Brooklyn girl, her fiancé, and the elaborate family shenanigans that take place before their wedding. The movie was *Moonstruck*, and it sure did strike, like lightning. Everything had come together, especially the cast: Cher, in the midst of one of her periodic career revivals; Nicolas Cage, at the start of a career full of great roles; and the great character actor Vincent Gardenia as Dukakis's husband. The movie had cost $11 million to make and took in more than $50 million, making it one of the top-grossing films of the year. The following spring, Dukakis and Cher were both nominated for Oscars—and won. Olympia's victory speech thanked all the usual characters, of course, but also included a shout-out to her cousin Michael, then in the thick of his run for the presidency. Had he won, we would still be talking about 1988 as the Year of the Dukakises.

Since then, she's worked steadily and well, in at least a few movies a year, and not always as someone's mom. Of particular note have been roles in Woody Allen's *Mighty Aphrodite*, as Jocasta (perhaps cast for her ethnicity as well as for her skill); in the well-regarded PBS series made from Armistead Maupin's *Tales of the City* stories; and in the long-awaited, much-delayed film of *A Confederacy of Dunces*. Perhaps inevitably, given her political family, she's been public about her beliefs, speaking often about women's issues with vigor and more than a little spice. "Yes, I'm a feminist," she told one audience during a recent speech, in response to a question. "What the hell else would a person with half a brain be?"

Greek Americans in Politics

It shouldn't come as a surprise that so many Greek Americans have succeeded in American politics. Contemporary Greeks have been through a lot in the past century, from Turkish attacks to Nazi occupation to civil war to a military junta, and all that instability has created a politically engaged populace. Besides, Greece has long been said to have a "culture of argument"—the spirited debate that takes place everywhere from cafés to parliament—that comes from deep within the Greek soul. Greek pride in American democracy—*we invented that!*—is likewise a powerful motivator. And let's face it: if you've ever been to a Greek family dinner, you know that a certain kind of Greek likes to tell everyone what to do.

Though his name became a bit of a punch line after the 1988 presidential election, Michael Dukakis remains an American political success story. Raised in Brookline, Massachusetts, by his immigrant parents, Dukakis was educated at Swarthmore College and Harvard Law School; by the time he was thirty, he was a member of the state legislature. In

1974, he was elected governor of Massachusetts, inheriting the state just as its economy was falling to pieces, and though he managed to turn things around, he was voted out of office in 1978. His successor was less effective at reversing the decline, however, and Dukakis ran again—and won—in 1982. Even his political opponents concede that his second stint as governor was an enormous success, marked by economic health and the beginning of Big Dig, the monumental (if financially messy) two-decade project devoted to rebuilding much of Boston's public infrastructure.

His reputation grew across the United States, and in 1988, Dukakis ran for president on the Democratic ticket against George Bush, the sitting vice president. His campaign got off to a good start, and he was generally perceived as a good and frugal leader at a time when many Americans were concerned about the federal deficit. For much of that year, Dukakis led in the polls; at one point in late summer, he was 17 percentage points ahead of his opponent. But his lead didn't last. Too many Americans viewed Dukakis as a dispassionate figure, one who couldn't energize the electorate, and the Bush campaign mounted several attacks that hurt his standing. One campaign ad, about a murderer named Willie Horton who'd been paroled under a Dukakis-backed program in Massachusetts and immediately committed several horrible crimes, was particularly effective. And Dukakis misstepped a few times himself. A campaign appearance in an Army tank, during which he donned an ill-fitting green helmet, produced a goofy-looking photo that proved useful to the Republicans, who were already trying to paint

Dukakis as a liberal ill at ease with the national-defense establishment. By October, his lead had evaporated; on Election Day, he carried only seven states. He spent the next few years finishing out his term in Massachusetts as another recession took hold, tarnishing his legacy.

Fortunately for him—and for Americans, for even if you disagree with him, Dukakis has led a blameless life as a corruption-free public servant—the governor has had a successful afterlife, particularly as a professor at Northeastern University. Today he often works on policy issues concerning reform of the health-care system. (Amazingly enough, four years after Dukakis's run, another Greek Massachusetts Democrat popped up in the presidential race. This time, it was the state's junior senator, Paul Tsongas, who ran a strong early campaign against Bill Clinton before he was overtaken in the later primaries. Clinton, of course, would ultimately beat him to the White House, aided by revelations that Tsongas had been less than forthcoming about cancer treatments he'd undergone before the campaign. In fact, he probably would have been too ill to serve; the cancer did return, and Tsongas died in 1997.)

Though Dukakis is the best-known Greek in U.S. politics, he's hardly the only one. Olympia Snowe of Maine was the first Greek American woman in the House of Representatives when she was elected in 1978, she and moved on to the Senate in 1994. A moderate Republican, she's known as a legislator who's willing to build bridges between the parties—aided by considerable personal charm—and valiantly did so during the impeachment trial of President Clinton. She's active on the Senate Finance Committee, one of the most powerful in the Capitol, and has been active in women's issues, especially those involving women in the military.

Across the Senate aisle from Snowe—and just a few seats away alphabetically—sits Paul Spyros Sarbanes, a highly respected Maryland Democrat, and Maryland's longest-serving senator ever (five terms and counting). He's the son of immigrants from Livonia who settled on the Eastern Shore of Maryland and opened a restaurant. Sarbanes, like Snowe, came to the Senate through the House of Representative, and he's particularly distinguished himself by co-sponsoring legislation, proposed after the Enron and Worldcom scandals, that goes after corporate misbehavior and accounting fraud.

Iannis Xenakis

If Yanni is the free-spirited, easy-listening goofball of Greek music, his polar opposite must be Iannis Xenakis. This formidable force of twentieth-century avant-garde composition produced work that is difficult, dissonant, and to some ears harsh—but it has influenced countless other musicians. His music is extremely abstract and driven by mathematics, and in fact, his schooling was not in music but in civil engineering. In a sense, his is an approach that the ancient Athenians would have appreciated. Logic and reason, by way of science, informed all their arts. Plato saw little distinction between culture and mathematics, and so it is with Xenakis.

His life was not easy at first. Born in Romania to Greek parents in 1922, he fought for Greece during World War II and then in the Greek resistance against the occupying British. While fighting that civil war, he was badly hurt by shrapnel in an incident that cost him an eye and left one side of his face badly scarred. Eventually, he settled in Paris, where he took a job as an aide to the great architect Le Corbusier and studied music on the side.

As he developed his own compositional voice, Xenakis grew frustrated with the prevailing avant-garde theory among serious musicians, a discipline known as serialism. It's difficult to describe serialist music without a pile of recordings, but the theory calls for the notes of the scale to be set in a predetermined order, replacing the conventional scale, and for that order to be maintained throughout a given piece. Its chief proponent was the composer Arnold Schoenberg; to the untrained ear, frankly, it can sound like a series of horrible mistakes.

Xenakis thought it a dead end and wanted to develop an entirely new music theory. His mathematical mind ultimately led him to a form he called "stochastic music," after *stochos*, the Greek word meaning "guess." (In mathematics, stochastic processes are those incorporating unpredictable, random actions, such as the fluctuation of the stock market or variations in temperature.) In stochastic music, the parameters like a pitch range are set, and then the piece unfolds with notes chosen at random—either through a mathematical algorithm or even, in some of Xenakis's pieces, by a computer.

The result can be harmonious or dissonant, lush and enveloping, or explosively clashing. And, like serialism, to those not in the swim of the avant-garde, it can be somewhat tough on the ears. But serious musicians, long since tired of working in familiar idioms, drank it up, especially those working in the new world of electronic instrumentation. Xenakis has been cited as a major influence by composers as diverse as

Pierre Boulez and Lou Reed. And there's definitely precedent for his work. Bach's fugues, after all, are extraordinarily mathematical in their precision. It is no surprise that Xenakis himself brushed away the criticism that his music was cold, admitting only that he rejected traditional sentimentality in favor of reason and intellectual heft.

Pete Sampras

There was a point in the mid-1990s when Pete Sampras almost seemed *too* good at tennis. He so dominated the sport, hammering balls back from the baseline with so much power and consistency before charging the net, that fans began to get bored with his game. The greatest moments for pro tennis have often been about rivalries—Jimmy Connors and John McEnroe, Martina Navratilova and Chris Evert—and for most of the decade, nobody was nearly good enough to beat Sampras with any kind of consistency. Players had to wait for him to fail, and he did not fail often. Andre Agassi seemed to spend his career reaching the finals of tournaments, then losing to Sampras. In fact, when a reporter asked Agassi in 1998 to name the top five players of all time, he answered, "Sampras, Sampras, Sampras, Sampras, and Sampras."

Sampras has a long list of credits to his name, but a few speak loudest: six straight years, and 286 weeks, for which he was ranked the No. 1 player in the world. Seven Wimbledon singles titles in eight years. And $43 million in prize money, not to mention endorsements, sponsorships, and all the other financial rewards that come with being one of the world's best athletes. He broke out early, turning pro at sixteen. From then on it was a headlong ride. Starting in 1990, the next decade, he won multiple titles at three of the sport's four major events, called the Grand Slam tournaments—those seven Wimbledon titles, plus five U.S. Opens, and two Australian Opens. (He was hampered only at the French Open, which has the odd clay surface that hurts Sampras's style of serve-and-volley play; he never got past the semifinals there.) His first U.S. Open win, in fact, came when he was nineteen—nobody, before or since, has ever won it so young.

Sampras grew up in California, as so many tennis players do (all that sunshine means a long practice season, as well as a culture of out-doorsy athleticism and plenty of tennis courts). He didn't come out of the country-club set, though: Sam Sampras, his father, was an engineer and a restaurant owner. His mother, who didn't come to America till she was twenty-five, was genuinely poor, sleeping on floors with her siblings and working menial jobs. As in so many immigrant families, Sampras got one thing in particular from them: the urge to win. He's often described as a little bit distant, internalizing everything, and he's said that his family is the same way; for example, he had to let them know that he'd like them to come and see his championship matches. (Early in his career, his parents would be too worked up to watch him—they'd go for long walks while he played. They learned of one major victory when they passed a TV set in their local mall and saw him holding up a trophy.)

That distance has contributed to the notion that he's a boring player. He isn't, though a casual TV viewer might get more out of the theatrics of a Jimmy Connors or Ilie Nastase than out of his cool mastery. But this reputation for remoteness may have been further reinforced by his private life, which is refreshingly uncomplicated. By all accounts, he's deeply competitive and driven but a cool-headed guy who works incredibly hard at his game, and that doesn't create much in the way of stories. (The occasional "controversies" have mostly been minor flaps that took on a new life in the press, like the time Sampras told a reporter he'd been relieved to be knocked out of the U.S. Open quarterfinals the year after his first win.) But he is not without inner fire. When he took the No. 1 world ranking for the sixth year in a row, it was the culmination of a hugely determined fight. As of October, 1998, Sampras had been ranked No. 2, and he knew that for the final push he'd essentially have to stay on the road, mostly in Europe, winning every possible tournament for the remaining chunk of the year. It was an incredibly demanding competitive situation, one that would never come around again and one that few people knew about. Sampras later admitted that the stress was causing his hair to fall out in clumps and that he came home in December "as mentally and physically tired as I've ever been." But he also came back with something else: that No. 1 ranking. Chances are—given that the sport is growing deeper, with a broader pool of strong players and fewer singular stars—that record will never be broken.

David and Amy Sedaris

He's probably the only Greek who will ever become famous for working as an elf. David Sedaris first came to public attention in 1994, when he published a short story called "The Santaland Diaries," which he subsequently turned into a piece aired on National Public Radio. It's an account of a December spent as a temporary employee of Macy's department store in New York City, herding children along on their annual visits to Santa, and—well, suffice it to say, that it's not a traditional piece of seasonal cheer. Kids vomit; parents curse; and elves and Santas grow cantankerous and mutter horrible things under their breath. It sounds misanthropic, but Sedaris has an exceptionally light touch, and the story is more antic than horrible.

It was also, as short stories go, a smash, and since then Sedaris has made a career out of mining his peculiar life for even more peculiar tales. (He did in fact work as a Macy's elf one year; how much of the story you believe is up to you.) Since the publication of *Barrel Fever*, the volume in which "Santaland Diaries" appears, he's continued to write about his everyday existence in fictionalized form, especially his very, very strange Greek American family in Raleigh, North Carolina. (Or was it very strange? Sometimes, when reading Sedaris's books, one gets the feeling that his upbringing was pretty conventional, that he's just setting down on paper the off-kilter point of view we have as children, when we half-understand what we're hearing and seeing.)

Take, for example, his story "The Fatty Suit." It's about his father, Lou Sedaris, and the obsession he has with his daughters' physical appearance. Lou gets it into his head that David's almost forty-year-old sister Amy has let herself go. To tweak him, Amy returns home for Thanksgiving that year wearing a theatrical fat suit, looking like she's gained fifty pounds. (She wears only the bottom half of the suit—the top was too expensive—so that she looks not only fat but misshapen.) What's amazing about the story is that it doesn't make fun of fat people and doesn't make fun of Amy for pulling such a stunt; the only one who looks ridiculous is their father, for being so caught up in her looks. Judging by David's stories, the Sedaris parents often suffered at the hands of their children—though, from the sound of things, they have earned every bit of their treatment.

Which brings us to his sister Amy. Though David grew famous first, Amy may have the more familiar face. Her performances—she says she dislikes the word "comedy" because it sets up an audience for plain old jokes—are extremely, wonderfully eccentric. Take her sitcom *Strangers with Candy*, in which she played a fresh-out-of-rehab thirty-seven-year-old who decided to go back and finish high school. She inhabited the lead character, Jerri Blank, just by twisting her face into an anxious mix of a scowl and an awkward, inappropriate smile. It said a great deal about Jerri, and at the same time completely differentiated her from Amy, as surely as an accent or a heavy makeup job would have. (Sedaris is—speaking of physical transformation—known for her odd collecting habits, including a shelf's worth of artificial limbs.) The two Sedarises collaborate now and then, especially on short plays, where they're billed as the Talent Family. For once, there's nothing ironic about that.

Greeks You Didn't Know Were Greek

Given the level of Greek pride out there, you'd think there wouldn't be anyone under this heading. But Greeks put a lot of stock in family names, and if one doesn't have an "-opoulos" or a "-nides" or an "-allas" at the end, its owner can sometimes miss out on the Hellenic party.

That situation is true even at the very top of the status world. The Greek royal family—now scattered or in exile, since the monarchy was abolished by public vote in 1974—is what's called a "cadet branch" of the Danish hereditary rulers, with the hardly Hellenic family name of Schleswig-Holstein-Sonderburg-Glücksburg. Because of the long tradition of diplomacy via marriage, many Greek princes and princesses were routinely married off to royalty in the rest of Europe, thus rendering their names as un-Greek as their bloodlines.

Take, for example, Prince Philip, the Duke of Edinburgh, and the husband of Queen Elizabeth II of Great Britain. He's of Danish and Burmese colonial blood; his last name, before he married, was Mountbatten. When he speaks, he sounds about as Greek as Winston Churchill. But Philip was born in Corfu, the son of the late Prince Andrew of Greece and grandson of King George I. His chief distinction during his wartime service happened to be in Greek waters during the Battle of Matapan, for which he received the Greek Cross of Valour from the Royal Navy. Philip adopted the family name of Mountbatten when he became a British citizen, around the time he married Elizabeth. (The Queen's cousin, the Duke of Kent, is also of Greek descent; his mother, Princess Marina, was the daughter of the King of Greece as well.) So the Greeks can plausibly claim Philip as one of their own.

Similarly, consider Queen Sofia, the wife of Spain's king, Juan Carlos. Her mother was named Frederika of Hanover, born in Blankenburg, Germany. The remainder of Sofia's immediate lineage is, again, almost purely Danish. And confusing things even further, both her parents are descendants of Queen Victoria. So how can the Greeks claim her? Oh, but they can, and do: Sofia was born in Athens in 1938 to the king and queen of Greece. Her younger brother, in fact, was King Constantine, Greece's last monarch.

Of course, not all the under-the-radar Greeks out there are royal. Take the actor Billy Zane, for example. Everyone who was a teenage girl, knew a teenage girl, or had to listen to a teenage girl in 1997 knows about him, because Zane was the nasty boyfriend of Kate Winslet in a little movie called *Titanic*. It's still the most financially successful film ever made, having taken in more than $1 billion at the box office, and it's by far the role for which he's best known, though Zane has worked steadily before and since, starting with a small role in the first *Back to the Future* movie, and more recently appearing in the successful *Morgan's Ferry* and *CQ*. ("Zane" is not a particularly Greek-looking name because it's been shortened; he was born William Zanetakos, Jr.)

Tina Fey didn't need to shorten her already very short name, but she, too, is Greek American (on her mother's side, that is; her father is Scotch-German), born in Pennsylvania. Fey, as every comedy fan knows, has become a star since she became the head writer on *Saturday Night Live* in 1999 and is often credited with waking up a show that had become rather mediocre. She's also the first woman in that post, a particularly notable achievement since the comedy world in general, and *Saturday Night Live* in particular, is widely described as an exclusive boys' club, complete with hazing. She also anchors the show's "Weekend Update" news segment and broke into the movie world in 2004 as the writer and costar of the very successful high-school comedy *Mean Girls*.

And if we started this chapter with the top of the elite social set, we'll end with possibly the loudest, brashest, crudest, most outrageous rocker alive. Tommy Lee, the madman drummer of the heavy-metal band Mötley Crüe, is the child of a Greek mom and an American serviceman. Born in Athens in 1962, he moved with his family to Los Angeles, when he was four, and grew up to become one of the most fearsome drummers in rock and roll. In recent years, he's been as famous for his lifestyle, his marriage to the bombshell actress Pamela Anderson, his ugly custody battles with her after their divorce, and—maybe most of all—that homemade videotape in which he and Pam were wearing nothing but their many tattoos. (Stolen from their house, the tape has become a best seller among the adult-bookstore set.) Maybe his behavior is not the sort of thing that incites the Greek heart to pride, but hey, fame is fame.

Aristotle Onassis

No matter what he achieved in his own life, Aristotle Onassis will forever be best known as the "O" in Jackie O. The self-made shipping tycoon with the golden touch for business and unquenchable thirst for deals made international headlines in 1968 when he married America's beloved widow. It was five years after President Kennedy's assassination, and four months after Robert Kennedy's death.

The Greek Orthodox ceremony was held on Onassis's private island of Skorpios in the Ionian Sea and was attended by Caroline, John, and several less-than-elated Kennedy in-laws. Overnight, the Greek islands became a jet-set destination. (And that in turn made Onassis even richer: he owned Olympic Airways.)

Most believe Aristo and Jackie entered into marriage with high hopes and even tenderness, but they quickly began to live separate lives: she in her Fifth Avenue Manhattan apartment and he on his legendary yacht. By the time of his death in 1975, they were married in name only, but Jackie issued this statement: "Aristotle Onassis rescued me at a moment when my life was engulfed by shadows. He meant a lot to me. He brought me into a world where one could find both happiness and love. We lived through many beautiful experiences together which cannot be forgotten, and for which I will be eternally grateful."

Onassis was born in 1900 in Smyrna, Turkey, and he became a refugee in 1922 with the rest of the Greek population, following the massacre and burning of the city. He fled to Argentina, where he hustled as a dishwasher, laundry worker, and switchboard operator, always looking for a business angle. He made his first million in the tobacco business, having mastered the art of using important people: he convinced Italian soprano Claudia Muzio to smoke in public, thereby creating demand for his product.

Soon after, he met Ingeborg Dedichen, daughter of a leading Norwegian shipowner, who helped him buy his first freighter. Finally rich, Onassis planned to get even richer. In 1946, he married Tina Livanos, daughter of a Greek shipowner and part of the establishment Onassis wished to thumb his nose at. She was seventeen, he was forty-six. Tina gave birth to their two children, Alexander and Christina, within a few years.

Meanwhile, Onassis was being dubbed "The Golden Greek" by the press. He invented the supertanker, engaging in one-upmanship with rival Stavros Niarchos. Nights were spent partying at El Morocco in New York, and late, late nights at his desk, plotting ways to increase the size of his fleet. With characteristic largesse that some called "vulgarity," he spent $4 million to convert a 322-foot Canadian frigate into the world's biggest yacht, the *Christina*.

When Onassis hosted opera's Maria Callas on a cruise through the Greek islands in 1958, a passionate romance erupted between the diva and the tycoon. The on-again-off-again relationship lasted for a decade, a staple of the gossip columns, until Onassis abandoned her to marry Kennedy. Like the Kennedys, Onassis suffered tragedy in his family. His son Alexander died in an airplane crash at the age of twenty-five. Many believe the loss crippled Onassis, who was already in questionable health, and sapped his will to live; he died just two years after his son.

His daughter, Christina, outlived him by just twelve years, dying at thirty-seven after a tangled life filled with health problems, four brief marriages, and heavy prescription-drug abuse. Her only child, Athina Onassis Roussel, turned eighteen in 2003 and inherited her grandfather's shipping empire—rumored to be worth $3 billion.

PART III

PLACES

Athens

Athens looms so large in Greece's history and present life that it is difficult to separate the two. But the capital is very much a place of its own, one that in many ways bears only passing resemblance to the rest of the country. Whereas most of Greece is rural and slow-paced, Athens is gritty and bustling. Small-town Greece is determinedly resistant to careerism or hustle, in a culture that values café-sitting and leisurely dining as a vital part of life; Athens is at its heart a city of commerce and business, the country's economic capital as well as its political center.

Europe's oldest major city is by far Greece's largest, with a population of about 1 million—roughly 10 percent of the whole country. (Attica, which is the larger metropolitan area including Athens and the port of Piraeus, has more than 3.5 million.) Archaeological digs tell us that people have been living there since the Paleolithic age, roughly twelve thousand years ago. Since much of the rest of this book speaks of the great age of Periclean Athens, there is no point in recapping the rise of the city-state here. But there is one important point worth making here about Athens: though it was not the world's first big city, much of what we think of as urban life comes from the Greeks. The omnivorousness and intellectual exchange that we ascribe to city dwellers—the idea that their lives revolve around the exchange of big ideas as much as around daily concerns—is a very Athenian image, going back to the dialogue method of teaching that Socrates used with his followers. So is the image of the city as a place where people from small towns go to test themselves—that is, where they go to seek fame, fortune, or other glory. In short, what we think of as urbanity is largely the way of life that evolved around Athens itself.

One must admit that modern Athens is hardly the shining marble city of the Periclean age. It suffers the woes of all modern cities, and to a degree, that makes it a difficult place to live. Because of its age, it's been hit particularly hard by the era of the automobile. The narrow streets are choked with cars, especially at peak hours, and—as Greek laws governing tailpipe emissions are not nearly as stringent as American ones—the air is thick with exhaust fumes. That makes for a very dirty city, and the poor air quality is even slowly destroying the marble monuments of the Acropolis, as the limestone dissolves in the acid rain. Athens also had the poor luck to undergo its biggest expansion in the 1960s and 1970s, an age generally known for its sterile, brutal architecture. As a result, many of the city's high-rises are profoundly ugly buildings—concrete hives that owe more to the balance sheet than to a designer's sensitivity. (And when they're streaked with auto exhaust, they look even worse.) Finally—and though it's hard to pin anyone down to specifics—

Athens' government is known worldwide as being deeply bureaucratic, sluggish, and (at least in the past) corrupt, although Greece's entry into the European Union was contingent on a fiscal cleanup that seems to have been remarkably effective.

And yet, and yet . . . in among the sooty concrete apartment blocks and honking horns, something happens to people in Athens. If they are from overwrought, high-tension places, they slow down enough to enjoy the day; if they are from small towns, they are enchanted by the urbanity of a European city, the culture of cafés, and the wandering urban strolls. And if they're from countries without a deep grounding in the past—this happens especially with Americans—they are simply dazzled by the way Greeks live so comfortably amid the fragments of their predecessors. That's especially true of first-time visitors to the *plaka,* the old market district of Athens, which is a crazy quilt of small streets and smaller shops, dotted with *kafenions* and other places to sit and eat or drink. The plaka has a few too many souvenir shops these days, but it retains a great deal of vitality and charm, speaking to a certain kind of daily existence that's rapidly disappearing as cities move faster and faster. Even though it's noisy and often inhospitable, people who visit Athens are still enchanted by the mellow yet urbane life it offers, one of continual moderate pleasures. And after all, it was Aristotle—an Athenian himself!—who advised "moderation in all things."

The Cycladic Islands

The Cyclades are what many people mean when they say "the Greek islands." They're named for their arrangement in a circle (*kyklos*, in
Greek) around the island of Delos, their spiritual center, said to be the
birthplace of Apollo. About twenty islands of varying sizes make up
the archipelago, and they are among the most heavily traveled by
tourists in all of Europe. That's because they have plenty to recommend
them for leisure: great beaches, lovely villages, plenty of ancient sites to
visit, and—since they're close to Athens and the ferries from Piraeus run
often—easy access. They're distinguished from the rest of the Aegean islands most obviously by their architecture: as they rise from the harbor,
they're covered by brilliant white stucco buildings, many with tile roofs,
making each island look like nothing so much as a pile of sugar cubes.

The most famous is probably Mykonos, and that's where we'll begin
our tour. It is certainly the island that best exemplifies the sugar-cube
aesthetic, and the locals maintain it thus for an excellent reason: it is a
huge tourist draw, and they do an excellent business by keeping it that

way. The biggest tourist spot of all is right at the main harbor of Mykonos Town, where a line of old-fashioned windmills stands. (A photograph of them has appeared on seemingly every Greek travel brochure ever produced.) The buildings date from the sixteenth century and are circular; the vanes are thin, connected at their outer edges by a cord. Virtually no grain is milled by wind anymore, of course, but they are certainly picturesque. And they are the real thing, spinning gaily in the Aegean wind, whether they're working mills or not.

For those of more contemporary sensibilities, Mykonos also has a vibrant nightlife, and clubgoers from all over Europe—especially gay men, though it's quite welcoming to everyone, as it's a rather tolerant place—come here to dance and drink, particularly in the warm months. The drawback of all this tourism is that the local flavor of the island is somewhat diminished: it's a little too manicured and pretty and too much like a stage set to be perfectly Greek. It's also quite expensive nowadays, since the wealthy weekenders of Europe and America are willing to pay top dollar—or pound or Euro—at the best resorts.

Once you branch out from Mykonos, though, the Cyclades vary widely, from touristy and well traveled to quiet and relatively rustic. Head to Santorini, for example, and you'll find lots of nightclubs, hot tubs, and expensive villas, filled with the weekending wealthy of Europe. That's because there's plenty to see, from a remarkably good little museum devoted to the local archaeological findings to half a dozen of Greece's better wineries. The smaller islands in the group, like Sífnos, were once rarely traveled, but lately they have become extremely popular and therefore crowded. On the other hand, a slight deviation from the usual package-tour path will land you on Sérifos, where livestock abounds, little English is spoken, and visitors—while warmly received—rarely get beyond the port city of Livádhi and its beach. No matter what kind of Greek experience you as a visitor want, it's probably somewhere in this tidy little island chain.

Crete

In some ways, Crete feels like it's barely part of Greece—it's large enough, and has had such a varied history of its own, that it seems almost as if it's an independent country. In fact, the island has been under several countries' control in the past few hundred years: the Venetians and then the Turks held Crete, which was placed under Greek control in 1913. Today it's one of the more popular tourist spots in the Mediterranean, especially the eastern portion, where activity centers on the city of Heraklion and the nearby beaches.

But it's the island's earlier history that really sets it apart, because Crete was home to—and how's this for a badge of honor?—the first civilization in Europe. Starting in the Bronze Age, around 3000 B.C., a society known as the Minoans flourished on the island, especially in the capital city of Knossos, which peaked at around one hundred thousand residents. Technologically, the Minoans could hold their own with anyone else in their world, trading across the Mediterranean with a fleet of ships. They were also that rare society that seems to have gotten along without much hostility. Until late in the Minoan era, over more than a thousand years of civilization, the island bears no traces of fortification, and virtually no weapons have been excavated. Crete was also a distinctly egalitarian place, promoting equality of the sexes.

We know the Minoans principally through the excavations of the palace at Knossos, which began in 1900 under the direction of an Englishman named Arthur Evans. He was a careful and thoughtful archaeologist for his day, but his field was in its infancy, and he got a lot of things wrong as he reconstructed the royal complex. (Tour guides today, as they walk visitors through the palace, spend an inordinate amount of time pointing at details and saying "this is all incorrect.") Frescoes were moved to where they seemed to fit the décor; rooms were labeled incorrectly; even the name given to the building isn't quite right. Though Evans called it a palace, it was more like an Egyptian or Sumerian temple complex. The room Evans called the "throne room"—principally because it centers on a big stone seat—was meant not for royalty but for the cult religion of the Minoans. (He made the classic mistake of filtering his findings through his own worldview—that of Victorian England, where class mattered more than religion.)

Although the site at Knossos is somewhat muddled, it's still a magnificent way to learn about ancient Crete, and several of its frescoes and other works of art are counted among the great Greek treasures. Best known, probably, is the painting of a practice called "bull jumping." A little like Spanish bullfighting, it was a death-defying sport practiced by young men and women: a bull would be released to charge at the participants, who would grab the bull by the horns and leap over the animal's back, doing a somersault. It must have been a spectacular thing to see, let alone participate in.

The complex at Knossos contains one more extraordinary first. Crete is a place known for extremes of climate, and some have suggested that Cretans therefore spent an unusual amount of time and effort constructing systems to enhance their physical comfort. Among other things, the ruins on Crete contain elaborate channels and pipes arranged to carry off Crete's annual heavy rains. Smaller versions of these systems, built with terra-cotta pipes, made their way into the houses of the citizens of Knossos, allowing wastewater to drain away into the public sewers. And one small room in the palace has conduits built into the wall that flow under an open seat set between two gypsum partitions. Yes, it's just what it sounds like: Crete is the home of the world's very first flush toilet.

Corfu, Ithaka, and the Ionian Islands

It's easy to think that the islands of Greece begin and end in the Aegean. That's where a lot of the ferries from Piraeus head, bearing tourists and weekenders. Besides, the Aegean is the sea that mainland Greece wraps itself around and, to a certain extent, defines itself by. But those are not the only Greek islands. Up the west coast of the Greek peninsula, in the Ionian Sea—the body of water separating Greece from Italy—is another archipelago. The Ionian islands look different from those in the Aegean: they are lush and green, where the others are white and stony, because they get more rain than the arid islands to the east. Like much of Greece, they've been conquered and reconquered, though instead of being pounded by the Turks, these islands were under the control of the Venetians for more than four centuries, then spent several decades as a British protectorate. (They were ceded back to Greece in 1864.)

The northernmost of these islands is probably Corfu, near the Albanian coast. The best known of the Ionian islands, it's called "Kérkyra" by the Greeks; the name Corfu is a mangled version of "Korfiou," meaning "twin peaks" and referring to the pair of mountains on the island. Corfu has been through a lot—the Venetians, then the British, then a great deal of damage resulting from Nazi bombing during World War II—but since the sixties, it has seen a great deal of tourist activity, which has brought money and attention to the island. In the early 1990s, the capital of the island, Corfu Town, saw substantial rebuilding, and it's now a smart and pretty place. The larger island to the south, Kefaloniá—long avoided by visitors—has recently opened up to tourists and other outsiders and has grown popular and similarly developed. (One set of longtime Kefaloniá residents has found the new attention difficult: the local loggerhead sea turtles, which lay their eggs on the beaches and have trouble dealing with the noise, boat propellers, and various disruptions brought by human visitors. Happily for the turtles, the government appears to be taking notice, and measures to protect them are beginning to be enacted.)

Ithaka, on the other hand, is very quiet, barely visited, and, if you're the literary type, one of the most storied places in the world, for the simple reason that Homer's epics play out here. The title character's island hopping in the *Odyssey* is centered on his trip home to Ithaka. (Odysseus also makes a stop on Corfu, where Homer refers to the inhabitants by their mythological name, the Phaiakes, named for the daughter of Poseidon.) Visitors to Ithaka today often find themselves looking for sites mentioned by name in the epic. Actually, a few do exist, such as the spring where Odysseus's pigs drank and the cave of the Nymphs, and guides will happily take you on a tour. Whether you believe that the provenance of these spots is the real thing, or whether it's manufactured to separate you from your tourist dollar is, of course, up to you.

Which brings us to one other island on the Ionian coast that's known for a famous former inhabitant. You can't visit the tiny speck of land called Skorpios; it's privately owned, one of the few Greek islands that can make that claim. But the entire world once wanted to know what was going on there because its owner was one of the richest men in the world: the shipping magnate Aristotle Onassis. When, in the late 1960s, he was romancing the widowed Jacqueline Kennedy, he often brought her there on his yacht, the *Christina*. It's also where they were married in 1968. Skorpios was his (and her) hideaway, a place where he could be king and she could get away from reporters and the memory of her first husband's assassination. Strangely enough, the odyssey that took an ancient war hero through these islands and the one that landed a beloved, wealthy American woman here with the unlikeliest of men somehow did have one thing in common: both travelers wanted to get home safe, and both, in the end, did.

Rhodes and the Dodecanese Islands

If you were to go by an unlabeled map, you'd consider the archipelago known as the Dodecanese islands part of Turkey, as it lies close by, and nearly within sight of, the Turkish coast. If you visited the Dodecanese in the early part of the twentieth century, you'd have found everyone speaking Italian, and justifiably thought that you'd found yourself in Italy. (You'd have been right, as a matter of fact; the islands were under occupation by the Italian government from 1912 to 1943.) But—and you knew this, because why else would they be in this book?—the Dodecanese are essentially Greek, with a population that's never thought of itself as anything else.

The name, of course, refers to the fact that there are twelve main islands in the chain (*dodeca* is Greek for "twelve," giving rise to our "dozen"), though quite a few tiny islets poke their heads above the water between the main landmasses. The largest, Rhodes, serves as a sort of capital, with the area's largest airport and various other services. The importance of Rhodes goes all the way back to antiquity, however, when it was a trading and military power, with a city, also called Rhodes, at its northern tip that's said to have topped one hundred thousand people at its peak. (You can read more about its history in the chapter of this book devoted to the Colossus of Rhodes.) The town of Rhodes also had an extraordinary medieval history; it was a walled city, conquered by four or five successive cultures, that finally ended up part of the Ottoman Empire after a siege in 1522 and 1523, where it stayed until the Italians came in four hundred years later. Several other towns on the island, like Lindros, have medieval castles as well.

Today Rhodes is among the most visited islands in the Mediterranean, probably because it has everything: a great beach culture, extraordinary town life, a pleasant climate (it is among the southernmost Aegean islands, and therefore has a long warm season), and excellent museums and archaeological sites to visit. The beaches are known in particular for their distinctive smooth, walnut-sized pebbles, and many streets in the towns of Rhodes and Lindros even have pebbled pavement.

A word here about the minuscule Dodecanese island of Hálki, which today is a very quiet place but is significant in the history of many American Greeks. A hundred years ago, Hálki was far livelier than it is today, with a population of several thousand and a thriving commercial life. Its economy was based on sponge diving—the longstanding tradition calling for young, strong-swimming men who dove to nearly superhuman depths. (In the old days, they did it with no air tanks, helmets, or anything more than lung power; today technology has made their jobs easier, though a few divers still do it the old way to maintain the tradition.) However, in the first few years of the twentieth century, a blight struck the area, killing off most of the sponges and destroying the business. Much of the population left, but rather than scattering, the divers and their families stuck together and headed for another place with warm water and the potential for a sponge-diving economy. Other Greek immigrants, from both the Dodecanese and elsewhere, soon joined them. As a result, the city of Tarpon Springs, Florida, is perhaps the most Greek spot in the entire United States, with a thriving Hellenic community and the attendant restaurants and other cultural amenities. And despite ups and downs through the years because of pollution and other threats, the sponge divers of Tarpon Springs still carry on their trade.

More recently, an even smaller Dodecanese island made international news. In 1995, a Turkish freighter ran aground on one of a pair of uninhabited islets called Ímia—barely more than two little stones sticking out of the sea off the coast of Kalymnos. A passing Greek ship offered the captain help; he refused, saying that he believed he was in Turkish territory and that he'd get help from his own government. (He accepted help from a Greek salvage boat a few days later, when none had come.) Strange that such a minor incident should explode as it did, but it's strange only when one forgets what a powder keg the relationship between Greece and Turkey continues to be. In the next few weeks, the two governments realized that the ownership of these tiny bits of land had never really been firmly nailed down in either nation's eyes. (Most documents seem to indicate that they're Greek, however.)

The mayor of Kalymnos sent someone over to plant a Greek flag; soon after, a visiting group of Turkish journalists pulled it down and raised a Turkish ensign. Over several weeks, tension grew to the point where Turkey sent soldiers to the island, and the Greek populace seemed to be supporting further escalation of the fight. It took some rather gracious diplomacy on the part Greece's president, Costas Simitis, to keep this essentially meaningless incident from blowing up into a full-scale war. The two sides more or less agreed to leave the matter undecided, and both went back to where they were before the fight started. And, no doubt, to where it will recur again, the next time some unfortunate tiny matter causes these two bickering countries to confront their shared, awkward history.

Delphi and the Oracle

You can have your psychic hotlines, your speaking in tongues, your Nostradamus. History's best show of predictive powers, hands-down, was the Oracle at Delphi. A supplicant—always male, as no women were allowed to consult the Oracle—would arrive at Delphi, bearing a request for guidance, and first took a bath at a nearby spring. (One did not consult the Oracle in a less than pristine state.) Then he would make his way up the side of Mount Parnassus, heading for the temple of Apollo itself. The path was lined with statues and various other offerings made to the Oracle, both in advance of and in gratitude for its predictions. On arrival at the temple, one would face the Pythia, the priestess of Apollo—a middle-aged woman from one of the local villages who was required to be of pure reputation.

She sat in a small room that was said to lie over a crack in the earth, from which, according to Plutarch's history of the place, vapors would rise, inducing in her a kind of trance in which she would rant and rave and spout predictive wisdom. It was supernatural and powerful, to a degree that no carnival fortune-teller will ever be able to convey, and it operated for nearly two millennia, from 1400 B.C. until the complex was shut down by the Romans in A.D. 381. Its reputation long outlived the Greek empire. Even in Elizabethan England, Shakespeare sent two of his characters in *The Winter's Tale* to consult the Oracle. It's no coincidence that the dome-shaped stone at the center of the Temple of Apollo was called the *omphalos* (Greek for "navel"): the Oracle was considered the center of the world.

And what did she predict? Many things, to be sure, that are lost to history: personal predictions of love and money, of success and failure. Only Apollo himself knows whether any of it turned out right, and in any case, the cryptic nature of the Oracle's responses makes them highly open to interpretation, in any direction. Take the Oracle's best-known pronouncement, which preceded the Battle of Salamis in 479 B.C. The Oracle predicted that the war between the Persians and the Athenians would "bring death to women's sons," and then added that the Greeks would be saved by "a wooden wall." (Whose sons, and what kind of wall, was left up to the Greeks.) Various interpretations led to various defenses: Some Athenians built an actual wooden wall, to keep the Persians out of the city; it was knocked down, and they were all killed. Others wanted to block off the city's harbor with a wooden structure, at least until they were reminded that the Persians could simply use their navy to bring in their army and take the battle onto dry land. Still others took the wooden wall to mean the Greek navy's fleet of ships, which did in fact fight back the Persian army, saving Athens and rendering the Oracle's ruling correct, at least as the Greeks chose to believe it.

Most scholars believe that the Oracle's predictions were sincere—that is, the whole thing was not a con game on the part of the priests. But what the Pythia was doing as she ranted is a matter of some debate. Some archaeologists hold that it was a kind of hypnotic state, induced by the power of suggestion and nothing more. The scientific view that the seismically active rock formations at Delphi were emitting intoxicating gases was, for a very long time, considered nothing more than a vivid legend. But a research team recently found that two fault lines do indeed intersect under the temple, and a hot spring does flow through there, producing ethylene gas, which could in fact induce euphoria if enough were to collect in a small underground chamber—much like the one in which the Pythia sat to make her predictions. Plutarch, it appears, may have got the story right after all.

Epidaurus

The city-state of Epidaurus was located on the easternmost "finger" of the hand-shaped Peloponnesian peninsula, about two hours south of Athens. In the ancient world, it was a bustling and much-visited place, especially around the fourth century B.C. because it housed the temple of Asklepios, the Greek god of healing. (His three daughters, Meditrina, Hygeia, and Panacea, all gave rise to English words—"medicine," "hygiene," and "panacea"—dealing with health and well-being.) As a result, it was where the sick and injured came, hoping for a cure. That may be because the area, like many in the volcanically active Mediterranean basin, has hot springs that are said to aid in the curative process. Visitors were particularly drawn to the temple itself, which was known for its magnificent sculptures and its excellent *tholos,* or rotunda. This large round structure was the work of the sculptor and occasional architect Polykleitos, about whose achievements you can read in the Sculpture chapter of this book; his elaborately sculpted Corinthian columns at Epidaurus were highly influential on other architects' work. Not much remains of the temple today, apart from its basement level, which takes the form of a small labyrinth, made up from three concentric circular corridors. That may be because many believed the temple—incorrectly—to be a treasure storehouse, and it's said that when pirates swept through the city in the early Christian era, they tore apart the building looking for its valuables.

What does remain nearly intact at Epidaurus, and today draws many visitors, is its spectacular theater. Like most open-air auditoriums, it slopes down into a shallow excavation, and it really does show us how many aspects of a Greek theater performance were similar to what our actors and directors still do, right down to the terminology. The forward part of the stage at the center is circular, and the seats wrap about three quarters of the way around it. That sunken circular platform is called the *orchestra*; today's musicians who are known by that term are so named because that is where they sit, in front of the rectangular main stage itself. (As Greek theater progressed, the chorus stayed down in the orchestra, and the plotted action took place behind it, on the stage—again, prefiguring the way musicals are handled in Broadway theaters today.) At each of the wings, a small portal allows the actors entrance and exit to the stage; this structure is called the *proskenium*, a term that survives in theaters to this day (in English it's "proscenium," and it refers to the arch defining the front edge of the stage, behind which the curtain drops).

The theater at Epidaurus is huge, with twelve thousand seats, about the capacity of a good-sized hockey arena today. (It was greatly expanded by the Romans, who built out extra rings of stone seats.) Despite its size, the acoustics are excellent: actors in the orchestra can make themselves heard even in the back rows without shouting. And you'll notice that I said "can make themselves," not "once made themselves," because the structure is, amazingly, a living cultural entity. Starting in the 1950s, the theater was restored to a degree that made it possible to host performances there, and on warm summer nights, ancient dramas and comedies take the stage (and the orchestra) once again. They have been a major success for eager and appreciative audiences: the experience of hearing 2,500-year-old words spoken, in their original language, in a structure that perhaps saw their premieres, is not to be underestimated. Audience members often describe it as a nearly religious experience, one that connects them to the ancient world like no other. Drama indeed.

Mycenae

It's hardly as well known, but for half a millennium, Mycenae, not Athens, was the great military and economic center of Greece. Beginning in about 1600 B.C., this city on the Peloponnese peninsula, about sixty miles southwest of Athens, was the capital of a Greek empire, reaching as far as Thessaly and out to the Dardanelles, that bore its name. The Greece that Troy fought against in the Trojan War, the Greece of the *Iliad* and the *Odyssey*, was Mycenaean Greece. Only Crete's Minoan civilization rivaled it for power in this era, and in fact, the two nations had a complicated relationship, competing for resources and supremacy, a battle in which Mycenae eventually emerged the victor, not the least because its culture was far more militaristic than the Cretans'. (In Greek mythology, the city was founded by Perseus, a heroic son of Zeus, after he had fought and killed the Medusa.) Skilled in metalwork, the Mycenaeans also produced flax, oil, and wool, and for more than two centuries dominated trade in the Mediterranean.

Much of what we traditionally thought about this civilization came from the Homeric odes, in fact, but beginning in the 1870s, excavations added greatly to our understanding. A German archaeologist named Heinrich Schliemann—the same man who excavated Troy, and a devotee of Homeric poetry—began to dig at the site historically believed to be Mycenae. His archaeological techniques were by today's standards crude and his conclusions amateurish, but he did bring up a wealth of artifacts and information.

Schliemann was the first to uncover the rock-shaft tombs in which the honored dead were buried, and one of them held an extraordinary complement of gold and other treasures. Schliemann thought it was a royal storeroom rather than a sepulchre and christened it the "Treasury of Atreus," after the father of Agamemnon, king of the Greeks at Mycenae's zenith. And on finding a hammered gold death mask in the tomb, he is said to have gasped, "Behold the face of Agamemnon!" To this day, the mask—by any name, one of the great artifacts of the ancient world—is often called "the mask of Agamemnon," though that's an entirely poetic attribution. All the same, much of what Schliemann dug up seemed to verify Homer's stories, which up until this point had been believed to be pure fiction. The walls of the city's fortress were discovered to be made of giant blocks of stone, far larger than one or two men could lift; they quickly became known as Cyclopean blocks, after the one-eyed giants who were said to have lifted them into place. The largest and most elaborate gate into the city of Mycenae, with a pointed arch flanked by two enormous stone lions, is perhaps the site's most recognizable monument.

Ironically, Schliemann was, in one faint echo, like Homer himself: the poet was composing his odes well after the greatest years of the Mycenaean Empire had passed, assembling a historical narrative as an archaeologist does, from bits and pieces. Around 1100 B.C. (the date is arguable), invaders from the north, said to be Dorians, bore down on the city of Mycenae. There may have been a siege; there were certainly fires and violence. Thus, the fall of the empire's capital ushered in the first of Europe's Dark Ages. It would be four hundred years until Greek civilization would begin to gather itself again, to begin what is now called the Archaic period, the precursor to the great period of Classical Greece.

Thessaloniki

Thessaloniki will always be Greece's second city, a step behind Athens. But in some ways, it is less a monument and more a functional city than the capital. It's prettier and better laid out. Its pace is more leisurely, though it does not fall short on nightlife or culture or history. And it is, by many accounts, a friendlier place to spend a day. In away, Thessaloniki is more *Greek*.

And at one point, it was, pretty nearly, the most powerful place in the world. The northern Greek province called Macedonia, after all, was the home base of the empire that under Philip II and then Alexander the Great reached through half of Europe and well into Asia. Vergina, their first capital, was located where Thessaloniki is today. Although the administration of the empire moved to Pella in the fourth century B.C., Thessaloniki remained powerful, and Macedonia's rulers were buried here (as was Philip, whose tomb you can still visit today). But its power did not end with the Classical period. During the Roman era lots of building took place in Thessaloniki, and in fact, most of the ruins and ancient structures one can see there today are from the early centuries of the first millennium. The most prominent of these, a tall, drum-shaped building called the "Rotonda," dates to the fourth century A.D. and practically tells the story of Greece itself: Built as a Roman tomb, it eventually became a mosque, complete with minaret, and today is an Orthodox church (not to mention a tourist destination).

Which brings us to the city's Christian era that, if anything, is more glorious than its earlier history. Thessaloniki was the second most powerful city of the Byzantine Empire, after Constantinople. St. Paul himself is said to have preached here, in the years A.D. 49 and 50, and founded the city's Christian community. As a result, its churches were numerous and dazzling, encrusted with gold and mosaic work. Even as most Greek cities withered—sacked by tribes like the Visigoths from northern Europe—Thessaloniki managed to hang on, eventually building a city wall to keep the invaders out. The nearby monasteries on Mount Athos house some of the greatest illuminated manuscripts and other Byzantine art of all.

Unfortunately, the modern era was tougher on the region. Along with the rest of Greece, Thessaloniki was exploited during the several hundred years of Ottoman Turkish rule. Finally liberated in 1912, the city was badly damaged by fire just five years later. And in the 1920s, the expulsion of millions of Greeks from Turkey had the same effect that it did in much of Greece: chaos, a population explosion, and, ultimately, some of the cultural richness for which it's now known. (Thessaloniki was the center for rebetiko, the popular music of the era that evolved, like the American blues, in reaction to oppression.) Rebuilt after the fire, the new and modernized city was dealt two more blows: Nazi occupation during World War II brought Allied bombing and the deportation of the city's substantial Jewish population, which never recovered. (Today the city's Jewish Museum remembers that population's contribution to Thessaloniki's history.) And a major earthquake in 1978 did quite a bit more damage. But the city has survived, even flourished, and now it's sometimes spoken of as one of Europe's great cultural places, an over-size college town—unsurprising, because it's home to the respected Aristotle University of Thessaloniki.

And the region has one other claim to fame as well, particularly in a country so bound up with its past. In 1959, excavations in the cavern known as the Petrolona cave (and sometimes as *Kokkines Petres*, or "Red Rocks"), not far from Thessaloniki, unearthed a Pleistocene-era hominid skull, somewhat similar to a Neanderthal Man's skull. It has been dated to seven hundred thousand years old, one of the oldest human bones ever found in Europe. We will never know his name, if he even had one, but we can say that Greece's second city was home to its first Greek.

PART IV

CULTURE

Democracy

Of all the great inventions of the Ancient Greeks, one stands alone. That is because its basic principle—which states simply that government should be in great degree controlled by the governed—has allowed virtually every other cultural advancement we take for granted to happen. Free communication, unrestricted art, and technological innovation: all these things take place far more readily in a self-governing society than under a monarchy.

Unsurprisingly, it did not come easily. In the sixth century B.C., most of the power in Athens lay with an elite class of wealthy property owners. The economy was heading downhill, and many citizens were concerned that (as had happened in other cities during tough times) a tyrant could seize power. The board that governed Athens, a council of nine archons (chief magistrates), appointed a tenth member to its ranks and gave him unusual powers to effect change. He was named Solon.

Very quickly, Solon established new principles of governance. First, he decreed that power should be redistributed based on wealth rather than birthright. To do so, he divided the populace into four classes, ranging from the wealthiest farmers to the *thetes*, or serfs. Under Solon's reforms, anyone from the top two classes could become an archon, anyone from the top three could run for Athens' four-hundred-seat legislature; and anyone at all could participate in the *ekklesia*, or public assembly, a sort of town meeting that regularly took place on a hillside. Anybody could also bring a case to court and serve on a jury.

By today's standards, Solon's reforms may seem rather limited, relying as they do on wealth. Moreover, women had virtually none of the rights men did. But this change was a turning point. It was the first time peasants had been given any chance to affect their rulers' actions, and these reforms provided the first glimmer of social mobility, whereby one could move from one class to another through work and achievement. Solon also granted remarkable rights to noncitizens, allowed certain skilled immigrants to become citizens themselves, and wiped out debts. Taken together, the new set of laws was referred to as *Eunomia* ("good governance").

Solon's reforms withstood substantial challenges, but after several unsuccessful attempts, a dictator named Peisistratos conquered Athens in 546 B.C. He did, however, recognize that the rights to which Athenians had become accustomed could not be withdrawn without incurring their political wrath, and left in place the main reforms Solon had instituted. Subsequent leaders recognized this principle even further. One in particular, named Kleisthenes, broke down Solon's class system into ten groups distinguished not by wealth but merely by where they lived. The

Athenian democracy that developed was, in its final form, perhaps purer than even the American system, where electors and legislators lie between the voters and their leaders.

Over time, Athenian politicians even found it convenient to encourage democratic reforms, since suggesting that the people be granted more power was an excellent campaign strategy. But under Pericles, democratic Athens was not to last. When Sparta conquered Athens in 404 B.C., the city-state returned to oligarchic rule. Self-governance would not achieve the same level of development until well after the Renaissance, across an ocean and on a continent that the Greeks never imagined to exist. Thomas Jefferson and the drafters of the United States Constitution were, like all educated men of their generation, deeply schooled in the classics and looked directly to the Athenian model for inspiration.

Greek culture has much to be proud of, but the creation of democracy stands above all. It is the principle that has affected the quality of life of more human beings than any other, allowing them, for better or for worse, self-determination. Even in its imperfection, it may well be the most important single idea in the history of the world.

Philosophy

Greek philosophy is far too big a subject to address with any kind of comprehensiveness in a brief essay. That's particularly true because, to the Greeks, philosophy meant far more than abstract thoughts about our place in the universe. The ancients drew no distinction between that kind of abstraction and what we consider hard science—the examination of the world around us, trying to figure out what makes up the world and all that's in it. The great Greek philosophers were logicians, physicists, mathematicians, and more, attempting to sort through what they saw using every possible tool available to them.

Greek philosophy can be said to begin with a man named Thales, who was from the small Ionian town of Miletus. He and his followers (primarily two, named Anaximenes and Anaximander) began with a question so basic that it seems impossible that nobody had formally asked it before: What is matter? What is the earth made of at its most basic level? Their answers were simplistic (Thales said everything boiled down to water; his students broadened that idea, to include air among the world's constituent parts), but the answer itself is less important than the idea behind it. For the first time, thinkers were addressing these questions, not by cooking up answers based on superstition ("it was the creation of the gods") but with ideas that came from reasoned observation.

Which brings us to the great philosophers of the Athenian age, beginning with Socrates. Socrates took that questioning method to its fullest bloom and, in fact, used as his basic teaching tool the techniques of bringing up widely held beliefs, carrying them out to their logical conclusions, and thereby deflating them, and consequently proving them flawed. Typically, he did so in a question-and-answer discussion with a student. Called the "Socratic dialogues," these one-on-one talks are still a basic tool in university teaching: a student comes in bearing a bit of his worldly knowledge, and his teacher asks him to consider it, bit by bit, deconstructing his belief piecemeal to see if it holds up.

Although his ideas can hardly be boiled down to one sentence, Socrates is best known for one aphorism: "Virtue is knowledge." The words did not mean the same thing to him as they do to us: "Virtue," to the Greeks, meant less about moral rectitude and more about efficiency and expertise within one's chosen field. But the idea was simple, and it colors our own civilization's thought to an amazing degree: know the underlying principles of your work and life—whether your idiom is philosophy, stonecutting, or anything in between—and you'll be better at your job and a better person.

Socrates paid dearly for his beliefs, which tended to challenge political opinions as well as scientific and logical ones. (He also irritated many in the educated class by consistently comparing them to their inferiors. High-born people would ask him what makes a good politician, and he'd insist on drawing an analogy based on what makes a good shoemaker—a tendency that the snootier Athenians thought demeaning.) His students loved him; their parents often considered him a rabble-rouser who turned their children against their materialistic beliefs. Eventually, he was tried and found guilty of "corrupting the youth and interfering with the religion of the city," whereupon he was sentenced to death in 399 B.C. He went quietly and gracefully, drinking a cup of hemlock and dying amid his friends and students.

Of course, since these discussions were in a teaching forum—traditionally, on a hill on the outskirts of Athens—they are lost to history; records of them exist in the writings of Plato, Socrates' most illustrious student, who wrote several of his own books in the same form, and in fact used Socrates as a character to provide the teacher's half of the discussion. But Plato was no mere acolyte. He took Socratic ideas much further, attempting to show a rational relationship between the soul, the state, and the universe. The Platonic system held that only the purest ideas and forms are truthful; for example, every physical object can be reduced to a combination of five basic shapes (the cube, the sphere, and so forth). Furthermore, he elaborated on Socrates' idea of reason and questioning as the route to the highest good. He also believed that philosophers should be the ones who ruled nations, since only they could see the largest picture and the long view.

As Socrates taught Plato, so Plato taught Aristotle, born in 384 B.C. Aristotle's works were even broader than his forebears' were, expanding more deeply into astronomy, physics, and earth science. Most of all, though, his works mark the beginning of the split between science and the humanities. (You need look no further than the titles of two of his books to see the divide: *Physics* is about the workings of the natural world, proposing that objects are made up of tiny bits called "atoms." *Metaphysics*—that is, "beyond physics"—is about the conceptual and logical.) In Aristotle's world, every object or person has an essence, a basic idea that should be taken to its highest level. Athletes should strive to be strongest or fastest; artists should attempt to achieve beauty at all costs. Most of all, Aristotle believed people should strive for the ideal of rationality because the ability to think things through is the essential quality that separates people from all other forms of life. It defines our humanity, and it defines the way most citizens of the world see their lives today. From childhood, we learn to ask *why* things happen as much as what they are.

Drama, Comedy, and Tragedy

It is not deeply remarkable that Greek plays have survived to the present day. The stories of many ancient cultures, in variously fragmented forms, linger through the centuries in one way or another. But what is truly extraordinary about the theatrical plays that evolved starting around 1200 B.C. is that they can still be performed, understood, and appreciated by audiences nearly three millennia later. Where Greek audiences laughed, we laugh; where they wept, we weep. Moreover, the conventions that the Greeks developed have remained remarkably constant. The stage is still surrounded by tiered seats; longish plays are broken into acts; songs sometimes interrupt the spoken narrative; and comedy often pokes fun at the pretensions of the powerful.

Though it developed into a civilized entertainment, theater began as something much earthier. At the beginning of Greece's development into a nation, tribal groups celebrating the god Dionysius—devoted to the pursuit of pleasure—would stage revels, in which they gave release to their emotions in a bout of drinking, dancing, and chanting. Eventually, these revels coalesced around a rite called a "dithyramb," performed by a large group of men accompanied by flutes and drums.

The ritual was popular for centuries, and eventually an Athenian named Thespis began to modify the dithyramb: he would step away from the group of singer-musicians (by then called the "chorus") on-stage to narrate or explain pieces of the story. He is believed to be the world's first stage actor, and to this day actors are called "thespians" in his honor. He was successful enough to develop another innovation that has come down to the present day—he took his company on tour. Other innovations, soon afterward, included the use of masks, which, like today's theatrical makeup, exaggerated facial expressions so they might be better seen from the back rows.

Before long, theater began to take its familiar forms. In the tragedies that developed rapidly as Athenian democracy fostered an atmosphere of free and questioning thought, questions of right and wrong were addressed in stories that served as parables. Beginning with the work of Aeschylus, the chanting of the dithyramb gave way to stories accompanied by the chorus, many drawn with historical characters. His most famous work, the *Oresteia*, is a three-part play that uses the story of the war hero Agamemnon, killed by his wife Clytemnestra, to address questions of morality and revenge. In perhaps the greatest of all Greek plays, Sophocles' *Oedipus* trilogy, every family dynamic is examined: parental love, independence, responsibility, destiny, and fate.

The other great form of Greek theater is comedy, and here again, the plays that come down to the present day are quite enjoyable to modern audiences. In Aristophanes' *Lysistrata*, women from warring states decide to deny their husbands sex until the men agree to a cease-fire. It's a moral tale, but it's also played for laughs, and much of the remarkably bawdy dialogue would not be out of place in a contemporary film. Menander, who followed Aristophanes, amplified the traditions, bringing in stock character types (the grumpy old man, for example) who remain staples of the comic form.

Theater went into a long decline after the fall of Athens, although it continued to be performed in Rome and, sporadically, over the centuries until it began to blossom again in Shakespeare's England. In contemporary form, of course, it has expanded into film and TV. But the ancient work still has power: After the attacks on New York in September 2001, the Broadway play that drew the most audience attention and critical acclaim was director Mary Zimmerman's new staging of Ovid's *Metamorphoses*—a Roman play drawing on Greek tales. That such an ancient work could bring together a fractious modern city in a time of grieving speaks eloquently of its beauty and enduring value.

Architecture

Certainly, there are significant buildings out there that *do not* refer to Greek architecture. The cathedral at Chartres, for example, is purely French; Japanese temples come very much from their own idiom. But all over the world, when architects are called on to produce something truly dignified, very august, or otherwise solidly important, they consistently reach for the architectural vocabulary introduced by the Greeks: columns, pediments, symmetry, and a perfect sense of proportion.

The earliest Greek temples—for it is temple architecture that produced these innovations—began simply, probably as wooden structures that were slowly and gradually rebuilt in marble. Right from the beginning, however, those structures were distinguished by their proportion and orderliness. Their structure comprises three basic parts: a foundation called a "stylobate," topped by supporting columns, which in turn hold up a triangular pediment and roof. The columns themselves are also divided into three parts, called the "base," "shaft," and "capital." Other than its fluting, the shaft of a Greek column is never decorated with carvings or inscriptions, as it would be in, say, an Egyptian temple. For the Greeks, the elegant structure was ornament enough.

Greek buildings developed into several distinct styles over the centuries. The first Greek columns were sturdy, sometimes almost stumpy, with a dish-shaped capital decorated with no more than a plain band or two. This form is called the "Doric order," and it saw perhaps its finest and most delicate expression in the Parthenon and its contemporary structures atop the Acropolis in Athens. As the Doric form evolved in mainland Greece, another shape, called the "Ionic" column, developed to the east, on the islands and in Asia Minor. Ionic columns are thinner, with fluting that is more refined, and a scroll-like top called a "volute." The bases and capitals of Ionic columns also tend to carry somewhat more carving and other decoration. (Much later, a third order called the "Corinthian" came into vogue. Its columns, which have leafy, elaborately carved tops, are more common in Roman buildings than in Greek ones.) In all cases, the edges of the roof and the pediments are decorated with sculpture, usually in a band running around the building called a "frieze." In a few extraordinary buildings, like the Erechtheum in Athens, the columns take an entirely different form—that of elegant drapery-clad women. It's often been remarked that they look pretty calm, considering that they're supporting tons of marble on their heads.

It may surprise modern-day viewers of Greek ruins to know that those lovely marble structures were hardly so austere in their day. Structures like the temples of the Acropolis were painted in bright colors, strong reds and blues and golds, to a degree that you and I would consider almost gaudy. (The colors made the buildings stand out crisply against the sky and provided bright backgrounds for the sculpture.) Only in the Renaissance, when European architects began to revive and reinterpret Greek forms, did they begin to be represented in pure white, simply because the ruins those architects were copying had been washed clean by centuries of weather. Ironic, then, that the Greek architects who so prized purity of form never saw the even purer tributes to their work built centuries later.

Mythology

Where to begin talking about such a large subject? The Greek myths—the set of stories, fables, and religious beliefs surrounding the gods and goddesses of ancient Greece—loom impossibly large in Western culture. Who hasn't heard a reference to the underworld of Hades, to the Midas touch, to the opening of a Pandora's box? Even the word "myth" itself is Hellenic in origin. To the ancients, the term *mythos* meant any kind of story, and *mythologos* a storyteller. Only later did they begin to distinguish between a factual story and one with fictional roots.

The Greek gods were said to be a family: They were born out of the marriage of Gaea, the goddess of earth, and Uranus, the sky. Uranus and Gaea's children (six giants called the "Titans," followed by six sisters called the "Titanesses," and then by three one-eyed Cyclopes) displeased their father, who treated them cruelly until Gaea told the Titans to kill their father. Five of the six refused, fearful; the sixth, Cronus, attacked his father, who fled, giving up his powers and leaving Cronus as supreme ruler of the universe. Cronus's son, Zeus, would grow up to take his place (again, by smiting his overbearing father). Zeus settled down atop Mount Olympus, a real mountain that is the tallest in Greece, its top almost perpetually shrouded in clouds. There, he would raise his own family, and, after all, where better for a celebrity to get away from it all and find some privacy?

The real purpose of these stories was, of course, to give reasons and shape to the unexplainable. Take the story of Prometheus, who wished to allow humankind the use of fire—a privilege said to be jealously guarded by the gods. Prometheus stole a glowing ember from the family home atop Mount Olympus and smuggled it to Earth, instructing humankind to keep it burning forever. For the ancients, this provided an explanation for the discovery of fire, information that otherwise eluded them. It also explained why they made burnt offerings: to appease the anger of Zeus, who was said to enjoy the smell of roasting meat. (Prometheus suffered for his gesture. Zeus had him chained to a mountaintop, where a bird of prey tortured him, ripping out and eating his liver. Because Prometheus was immortal, the organ would grow back every night, only to be eaten again the next day, a process that would continue eternally.)

Zeus remained angry with the people of Earth (the stories say), and in another gesture of revenge sent them Pandora, a beautiful young woman whom he endowed with the flaw of hopeless curiosity. He then gave her a sealed box and told her never to open it. Of course she did; when she lifted the lid, it immediately released miseries on the world: greed, vanity, envy, lying, gossip, drudgery. All that remained in the box, when she slammed the lid back down was hope.

There are more stories, many more, and they certainly should be appreciated as literature. But more important, they allowed a people whose science was still only modestly sophisticated a way of understanding what they saw. The images were graspable ways of making sense out of a difficult world.

Sculpture

Let's begin with the marble. (After all, that's what the artists do.) In the quarries to the north of Athens exists a white limestone that's different from all others. It's called "Pentelic" marble, after the nearby Mount Pentelikon, and it's distinguished by its very fine grain and lack of veining and color variation. That is, it's totally uniform and smooth, and very, very white. Moreover, its surface is translucent, so light striking its surface penetrates a bit, to be reflected back by the internal crystals of the stone—in other words, it glistens, just slightly, in the light.

With such a resource nearby, how could Greece fail to produce master sculptors? And it did, beginning with exaggerated, almost tribal statues on the island of Crete around 3000 B.C., and rising to its full flower in Periclean Athens around 400 B.C. As their skills at stone carving developed, Greek artists mastered other materials, especially bronze, which, because it was expensive, was often used for special works.

The large human figures that to many people represent Greek sculpture are most important for the huge leap they represent in the observation of the human body. Look at earlier sculptures, Greek or otherwise, and the figures stand square, their weight evenly distributed on their feet, and their hips are at exactly the same height. Even when they are accurate representations of individuals, beautifully modeled, they look strangely formal and distant, not quite human. But if you stand before a mirror, you'll see that you don't naturally pose that way. Usually, one leg is held stiffer than the other is and bears more weight, with your hip dropped slightly; the other, ever so slightly bent at the knee, balances but does not carry your weight. And Greek sculpture began to capture this quality repeatedly.

That sounds like a small distinction, but it's fundamental to the artists' way of thinking. Rather than representing people crisply, as *ideas* of people, the Greek mind wanted to represent flesh and bone as it really appeared. (All the same, the subjects remained highly idealized: You'll rarely catch a Greek sculptor depicting a pimple or a bald spot.) Athenian figures have weight, defined muscles, and clothing that drapes like real fabric. The artists also display their reverence for the body, constantly rendering youthful, muscular men and women, either nude or wrapped in wet, clinging drapery to display every curve. Over the several hundred years in which ancient Greek society flourished, sculptors gradually grew bolder, making their statues even more lifelike and drawing subjects from all aspects of life and mythology, their poses evermore naturalistic.

The most famous Greek statues are unsigned, so the names of many of those sculptors of antiquity are lost. We do not know, for example, who was responsible for the spectacular statue of Nike, the winged goddess of victory, that was dug up on the island of Samothrace in 1863 and now stands in the Louvre museum in Paris. (If only for the feathers on the wings, its creator deserves immortality.) The even more famous Venus de Milo, just down the hall in the Louvre, is similarly anonymous. But a few Greek sculptors' names have come down through the ages, and their works (or, usually, Roman copies of them, made centuries later) can be identified with some confidence. Phidias, born in about 500 B.C., was generally acknowledged to be the greatest of his time. He was most famous for the larger-than-life gold-and-ivory statue of Athena that occupied the altar of the Parthenon, as well as the figures adorning the outside of the building, which are now known as the Elgin Marbles. (The statue of Athena no longer exists, though a few copies hint at its nature.)

Polykleitos, born about fifty years later, specialized in a sturdier, more athletic figure, and was renowned for his sense of human proportion. And finally, Praxiteles, born in about 400 B.C., gained fame for his expressive faces and finely polished marbles. His slenderer, smoother, more refined bodies constitute a high-water mark for Greek statuary, and one that—for the admiring Romans, for the Renaissance sculptors like Michelangelo, and even to figural sculptors of the present day—many artists consider a near ideal.

Ceramics

Every society develops its own ceramics—after all, we all need something in which to hold our dinner or store our water. And most societies, from the Navajo Indians to the Ming-dynasty Chinese to the varied cultures of central Africa, refined those utilitarian objects to make something beautiful. The Attic Greeks were no exception. A few basic forms developed to serve various purposes, like the amphora, a two-handled, narrow-necked vessel that became the standard shipping container of its time. Thousands have been found in seaport towns and in shipwrecks, where they held products such as wine or olive oil. Other shapes, like the tall, thin *lekythos*, used as a pouring flask for oil, and the *krater*, a vessel for mixing wine and water, served their own purposes.

But although their painted figures began as decorations, the images on Greek vases gradually evolved into something very different—not ornament but literature. That is, the figures posing, dancing, and gesturing their way around the belly of a Greek pot tell a story or record a historic event. They also demonstrate, like Greek sculpture of the same period, an increasing artistic awareness of the way the human body moves. They are collaborative works, since a potter made a vase that a painter then decorated, and one or both artisans signed quite a few of the best examples, allowing scholars to trace styles through the work of individuals. An excellent example known as the François vase has seven bands of decoration covering its surface, populated by two hundred painted figures depicting the wedding of Peleus, the father of the mythical hero Achilles, along with several other tales.

Two basic styles of decoration eventually developed. *Black-figure* ceramics are brick-red vessels on which images were painted in a glaze that through a complex firing process turned black, contrasting with the background. Later examples switch the color scheme, using dark glaze for the background and delineating the details in red; as you might expect, that style is called *red-figure*, and it allows greater expression, since the painted details stand out better against the background. Amazingly, we can trace it to one artisan. Though his name is lost, he is known as the Andokides Painter because the potter Andokides signed the vases he decorated. Later ceramic artists—Euphronios, Euthymides, and another known as the Brygos Painter—refined the way these visual stories were depicted. Again mirroring the development of Greek sculptors, they gradually grew better at realistically showing the figures' anatomical structure and the way people move.

The larger and more elaborate vases were decorative pieces. (After all, no one was likely to order a huge and finely decorated pot and proceed to bang it around in the kitchen.) Some of the most impressive served one purely ceremonial function: a wealthy Athenian would sometimes order an enormous vase, perhaps five or six feet tall, to serve as a grave marker. Its bands of decoration, rather than depicting mythological scenes, are sometimes purely geometric. Some display scenes from burial processions or scenes from the life of the deceased, and many are extraordinarily beautiful.

The Colossus of Rhodes

In 305 B.C., the city of Rhodes, the capital of the island of the same name, was under attack. A Macedonian tribe called the "Antigonids" held the city under siege and were held off by the ingenious Rhodians, who built a moat and vigorously defended their town. It took a year, but eventually, the two sides agreed to a peace. The Macedonians left, leaving behind heaps of swords, armor, catapults, and other military gear. To celebrate the end of the war and give thanks, the people of Rhodes decided to create a statue of the god Helios, who represented the sun. And build they did: They melted down all the leftover war material and cast an enormous figure, shading its eyes with one hand and topped with a spiky crown evoking the sun's rays. (Some accounts say the other hand was held aloft, holding a torch, to serve as a lighthouse.) Its skin was bronze; the interior skeleton was iron, supported by stone pillars inside the statue. And it was huge. By most modern figuring, it stood 110 feet high, on a 50-foot stone pedestal.

We have no ancient drawings of the Colossus, only descriptions, so every picture of the statue incorporates some guesses. But one popular image is probably incorrect. A great many drawings of the Colossus show it with one foot planted on either side of the harbor, as ships pass under its legs. It is a vivid and dramatic idea, but almost certainly wrong. None of the descriptions by Greek historians who saw it say anything about such a pose, and it would have been impossible to construct without shutting down the harbor for a very long time. Nearly all scholars agree today that it probably stood with feet together like most Greek statues, at one side of the harbor, facing the incoming ships.

The architect was a man named Chares, from the nearby town of Lindos, and what's known about him suggests that he came to a sad end. He probably didn't live to see the statue finished; some accounts say he killed himself, distraught over flaws in his masterpiece or money troubles. But his work achieved great fame, ranked by Herodotus among the Seven Wonders of the Ancient World.

It did not last long, however. In 226 B.C., just fifty or so years after the Colossus was completed, a major earthquake struck Rhodes, toppling the statue, which broke off at the knees. Its shattered parts were too badly broken to be reconstructed. (Besides, the citizens of the city felt that their pride might have offended the gods, causing them to shake the earth in anger.) Incredibly, the bronze fragments of the statue lay where they fell for eight hundred years, until Rhodes fell to the Arabs. In the year A.D. 653, a Syrian Jewish scrap-metal dealer bought what was left. It is said that it took nine hundred camels to haul it all away.

The idea of the Colossus, celebrating toughness and survival, lasted far longer than the statue itself. In 1876, another country known for advancing democratic ideals erected an enormous torch-bearing statue, wearing a spiky crown of sunbeams, for its principal harbor. Dedicated ten years later, in 1886, the Statue of Liberty greeted generations of immigrants arriving in New York by ship. (Amazingly, given the technological difference between our eras, it is not all that much bigger than the Colossus of Rhodes, at 120 feet tall, though the pedestal is much higher.) Lest anyone miss its relationship to the ancient wonder of Rhodes, there's a clue in the famous Emma Lazarus verse ("Give me your tired, your poor. . . .") inscribed at its base. Though every schoolchild knows the poem, fewer know its title: "The New Colossus."

The Marathon

The story of the marathon that students learn is romantic and straight-forward. After the Athenian army overwhelmingly defeated the Persians at the Battle of Marathon, in 490 B.C., the fastest available runner, named Pheidippides, was sent back to Athens with the news. Already exhausted from the battle, he ran the twenty-six miles in record time, announced the victory (*"Nike! Nike!"*), and immediately fell dead. When the Olympic Games were reinaugurated in 1896, a race of the same length was created in his memory—and, amazingly, a Greek runner won the event that first time.

As with so many tidy stories, the truth is a little murkier. Yes, Pheidippides was an Athenian soldier known for his speed, and he did fight at the battle. But the best history we have, written by Herodotus, simply says that he was sent off to Sparta before the fight, asking for re-inforcements. (Mind you, that meant running a truly heroic 145 miles in two days.) But, adds Herodotus, the whole army returned to Athens after the battle, not just one runner. A later historian did suggest that a single messenger returned to Athens with the news and died, and later writers seem to have picked up Pheidippides' story and melded the two.

What is certainly true is that the popularly known story—correct or not—is responsible for the existence of the race we call the marathon today. At the first modern Olympics, in Athens in 1896, the run was, in fact, set up on the route thought to be Pheidippides'. (Slightly shorter, actually: the length was rounded off to forty thousand meters, or about twenty-four miles.) There were seventeen entrants (thirteen of them Greeks), and although all were runners, they were hardly the elite, superbly trained athletes we know today. Three of the four non-Greek runners had never run a race of that length before. The local athletes, on the other hand, had been training on the course for a couple of months.

So it is perhaps not surprising that just under three hours into the race, when the first runner arrived in the stadium at Athens's Syntagma Square, the roar came up from the crowd: *A Greek!* His name was Spyridon Louis; his time, 2 hours, 58 minutes, 50 seconds. (His time might have been a little quicker had he not—and this is not a joke—taken a break for a glass of wine in the middle of the race.) Second and third places also went to Greeks, though the third-place runner, Spyridon Belokas, was eventually disqualified for cheating. He had hopped on a horse cart for a portion of the distance. His medal went to the fourth-place winner, a Hungarian named Gyula Kellner.

The controversy soon evaporated, and something lasting did come out of that first modern marathon. In the first Olympic Games, as today, the wealthier Western nations, like Britain and the United States, took the lion's share of the medals, and some of the enthusiasm was drained from the Games because of the lopsided result. Spyridon Louis's victory revived the spectators' flagging enthusiasm, whipping them into a bit of nationalistic excitement. The drama provided a great news hook, giving the fledgling Olympic movement the momentum it needed in its fragile beginning—kept the flame going, if you like. His success, in a small way, may be the reason the Olympics still exist today. *Nike*—victory!—indeed.

Archimedes and the Greek Scientists

It is, admittedly, wrong to say that the Greeks were the first scientists. Primitive man learned to manage fire, domesticate animals, and advance agriculture; the Egyptians had a remarkable set of well-developed practical sciences, especially engineering, long before classical Greece came into being. But the lion's share of the early theoretical work in physics, chemistry, mathematics, and astronomy took place in Greece.

Their concrete achievements aside, the fundamental creation of the Greek scientists was something perhaps more important. The Greeks were the first to formalize the process of hypothesis and experiment: the idea was that to find out things about the world, one should make observations, form a theory based on them, and test it. If it works, the theory is proven, and one can proceed; if not, back to the drawing board. It's the basic procedure without which no science can advance; it's also less obvious than it seems. (Even today, too many people, in the sciences and elsewhere, create a theory, then choose their facts selectively to get the answers the want.)

Consider, just for example, the works of Archimedes. Born in the Greek city-state of Syracuse, in present-day Sicily, Archimedes was fascinated by pure mathematics and its practical applications alike. He was the first to figure out, among other things, how to compute the surface area of a sphere, having proved its relationship to that of a cylinder. (He even wrote a book with the catchy title *On the Sphere and Cylinder*.)

But it is his practical work for which he's often cited today. Most famously, the king of Syracuse once asked Archimedes to inspect a gold crown he'd had made. The king suspected that the smith had set aside some of the gold to sell and cheapened the crown with lighter metals. However, there was a catch: he couldn't cut into or otherwise damage the crown to evaluate it. Archimedes studied the problem with no solution until he was settling into his bathtub one day and saw the water level rise—whereupon he leapt from the tub and ran naked through the streets of Syracuse shouting "Eureka!" ("I have found it!"). What he'd found was the principle that an object dropped into water displaces exactly its own volume. So Archimedes asked the king for a lump of gold exactly the same weight as the crown; the crown, submerged in a basin, raised the water level more than the solid gold did, proving the goldsmith to be crooked.

Much of his work was devoted to building war machinery. Legend has it that he used giant bronze concave mirrors to focus sunlight on the enemy's approaching ships, setting them afire. He codified the principle of the lever, allowing the building of catapults and inspiring his famous saying, "Give me one firm spot on which to stand, and I will move the earth." He conceived the first helical propeller, still called an "Archimedes screw." And based on his observations of celestial bodies, he built a complex mechanism that showed the movement of the planets— the world's first planetarium.

His sad death was recorded by the Roman writer Livy. When the Romans took Syracuse in 211 B.C., the leader of the invading troops, Marcellus, called for Archimedes to be brought to him alive, out of respect for the designer of the war machines he'd had a hard time overcoming. A Roman soldier burst in on Archimedes, who had been so wrapped up in his work, it's said, that he hadn't noticed the invading army. Engrossed in the diagram he was sketching in the dust on his floor, he didn't respond to the soldier's demands; when the soldier finally threatened him, Archimedes, still distracted, gestured to the diagram and admonished the young man, "Don't disturb my circles." The soldier, irritated, ran the old scientist through with his sword, causing him to fall on and obliterate the very work he wished to protect. Marcellus, on hearing the story, arranged for a respectful burial in a tomb topped with a marble cylinder and sphere, to mark Archimedes' most significant mathematical work.

Medicine

As in philosophy and mathematics, the Greek desire to understand the world through observation and logic brought about giant leaps in medicine, and the most influential ancient approach to medicine came from the works of Hippocrates. We know little of this physician's personal life, beyond that he was born on the island of Cos in the fifth century B.C. (It may well be that he was not one person but a number of teachers whose works had been combined.) But the school of thought surrounding his work made for the first giant leap in the history of medicine: the idea that superstition and philosophy were largely to be disregarded and that scientific observation and analysis were the source of knowledge.

Hippocrates' basic contribution was to apply the theory of the four Platonic elements—fire, air, earth, and water—to the body itself. In Hippocrates' view, for example, the heart and circulatory system corresponded to fire, keeping the body hot and vital; the respiratory system kept that system cool, relating as it did to air. He further held that the body's operation depended on four fluids, related to those four elements: blood, phlegm, black bile, and yellow bile. These substances, called "humors," were responsible for all aspects of one's personality, health, and well-being, and an imbalance in their production would cause illness. Too much phlegm, for example, would turn a patient sluggish, whereupon Hippocrates prescribed citrus fruits—which, because they contain sugar and vitamin C, may well have perked up his patients.

Of course, this theory is by today's medical standards not very sophisticated. Nonetheless, its basic tenets have correlations in modern medicine. Though we know that the body's chemistry is far more complex than Hippocrates realized, doctors do approach basic diseases somewhat the same way: examine the patient; look at what is out of whack; diagnose; prescribe. The notion of clinical observation as a route to cure is largely Hippocrates' own. That may be why doctors to this day, when finishing medical school, take a modified version of the oath attributed (questionably, but no matter) to him.

Hippocrates is known today as "the father of medicine." But the greatest physician of the ancient world may have been Galen, born several generations later, around A.D. 130, in the years when Greece became a Roman colony. Galen's works build substantially on that of Hippocrates, and in fact quite a bit of his writing is commentary and elaboration on his predecessor's. Among other works, Galen's research included detailed studies of the function of the spinal cord and the internal organs like the kidneys; he also introduced the idea of dissecting cadavers to learn more about the body's internal function. His fame grew quickly, eventually gaining him a post as the Roman emperor Marcus Aurelius's personal physician.

Galen's work, in fact, ended up being quite a bit *too* influential. After the fall of Rome and throughout Europe's dark ages, the scientific methods of the Greeks—observe, hypothesize, test—fell into disuse. But Galen's research survived, particularly in the Arab world, where it was faithfully studied even as Europe's culture disintegrated. Rather than building on his discoveries, the less sophisticated doctors of the medieval era treated his work as almost holy; where it failed to match up with the facts, and even sometimes was flat-out incorrect, the observations were discarded, and medical progress essentially froze in its tracks. It took 1,400 years until the doctors of the Italian Renaissance began to suggest that one might question the ancient works rather than simply taking them on faith, and only then did research catch up with Galen. His textbooks continued to be used, not as historical material, but as actual working medical manuals, well into the 1800s.

The Greek Language

Before we begin talking about the Greek language, we must settle on which Greek language we mean. Modern Greek, of course, is the everyday language of contemporary Greece; ancient Greek is the language of Homer, Pericles, and the writers of the New Testament. But even if that distinction is observed, the question, "What is Greek?" is not so easy to answer.

The ancient Greeks didn't have just one language, and of course we don't know exactly how they spoke; we only have their written texts and very little to go on when it comes to pronunciation. That record begins for us around 1200 B.C., on the island of Crete, where it began to appear on clay tablets. It's not an alphabetic language; it's written with pictographs for each syllable, rather like Chinese characters. It's called "Linear B," and it was the language of the Mycenaean culture, both in Crete and on the mainland. The tablets were first dug up in the 1870s, and the language eluded translation until 1953, when Michael Ventris— through the use of a series of grids that associated the symbols on the tablets with consonants and vowels—unlocked the text. (Another language from roughly the same period and place, probably adapted from Linear B, is called "Linear A," and remains untranslated to this day.)

As the Mycenean civilization gave way to the classical period, the languages of Greece varied by region and people in many dialects. But the forms that developed on the coasts of the Aegean would eventually become a sort of standard. The Athenian form was called "Attic"; the form in Asia Minor was called "Ionic." The two eventually blended, and Attic-Ionic, the language of the literate era in Periclean Athens, is what we generally think of as Classical Greek today—the language of Plato and Aristotle.

More change was to come, however. As the Greek Empire grew and reached all around the Mediterranean, Greek, like English today, picked up new words, new grammatical idioms, and new slang. The language that developed was much more populist than Attic-Ionic, so much so that it has another name. Called *koine*, it's the language in which the New Testament of the Bible was written and in which some of the Greek Orthodox liturgy is still conducted. It was also frowned on by the educated elite, who found Attic the more elegant form of the language, rather like the way the British tend to look down on American English.

Which leads us to Modern Greek, for a similar distinction exists today. As Greece emerged from Turkish domination, becoming an independent country once again in 1821, intellectuals throughout Europe offered suggestions for a national language. What emerged was a compromise—not Attic Greek, as some high-minded folks suggested, and not a codified form of the Greek spoken by peasants at the time, but a pair of languages. *Katharevousa* would be used for literature and other formal communication, and *demotiki* would serve for everyday communication.

As you might expect, the distinction got rather blurry, not to mention confusing, before long. (Imagine the mess if, in America, all formal communication and news were conducted in British English, whereas everyone spoke in a strong Southern drawl.) Inevitably, the elite dialect began to be contaminated by popular phrases and words. By the late twentieth century, a few documents and one Athenian newspaper were still written in *katharevousa*, but nearly everything else was in the more popular *demotiki*, and in 1976, the latter officially became the language of government documents and education. Though fragments of its more formal sibling survive in everyday use as needed, *demotiki* has effectively won out, and for the first time in centuries, most Greeks speak the same language, which they simply call the *glossa*, or mother tongue.

The First Historians

One might think that recording events for future generations would be the first form of writing and so obvious that it would not need to be invented. But that is not so. Civilizations before the Greeks recorded things they needed, such as financial records and agricultural data, and wrote down material such as prayers. A few writers put together lists of historical events, in very dry works that were more time line than tale. It took the Greek curiosity about the past, and a sense of story, perhaps unsurprising in the culture that gave us drama, to invent a new genre of writing: historical narrative.

And that begins with Herodotus, born in the fifth century B.C. His nine books, which today are usually presented in one volume called *The Histories*, constitute by far the best record of the ancient world up to that point. Herodotus meant to record the war between the Greeks and the Persians. In the process, however, he did what any good historian would: he began to research the background that led to the conflict. He traveled throughout the Mediterranean basin and throughout the

Middle East, taking down remembered stories and taking notes on what he saw. He was an excellent journalist, faithfully rendering various points of view in an entertaining narrative that's surprisingly readable today.

It's no criticism of Herodotus to say that many of his facts are a little shaky. He did a remarkable job, considering that he couldn't rely on any previous records; as one historian has put it, imagine writing a history of World War II, several decades after the fact, without any newspapers or books as sources. It would be a huge task, and the result would be riddled with conflicting stories, disparate points of view, and plain old errors. So it is with Herodotus's histories. Take, for example, his account of the building of the Great Pyramid of Giza, in Egypt, in which he says that construction required one hundred thousand men and twenty years. Herodotus probably went to Giza and asked locals for the story—never mind that the pyramids were already two thousand years old when he got there. Naturally, they treated him as any small-town folks would anywhere: they exaggerated, whether out of ignorance, pride, or a desire to pull his leg. But what they said went into the book, and those figures, being the closest we have to a contemporary account, are often still quoted today, though modern estimates are far more modest than his.

The other great Greek historian, coming a generation after Herodotus, was Thucydides. Of his work, one book survives, a history of the Peloponnesian War between Athens and Sparta. Thucydides had, in fact, been a general in the Athenian army—and an unsuccessful one at that; when he contributed to the loss of a major battle, he was thrown out of Athens and spent the rest of the war writing rather than fighting. Unlike Herodotus, he takes a strong point of view, presenting information analytically, using the events of the past to teach about the future. He also gives excellent accounts of the war itself and the subsequent fall of Athens, which he blames on imperialistic overreaching (especially the attempt to conquer Sicily, which stretched resources too thin and left Athens vulnerable). And he records some of the most stirring words of his time: the funeral oration given by Pericles to honor the war dead. It was the Gettysburg Address of its time, a speech eloquently eulogizing those who have died for a greater good. Most of all, however, Thucydides explains that he studies the war so that subsequent generations might at least understand it and, in doing so, take steps so that war might be prevented. To this day, that's the driving force behind most historians: if we can understand our mistakes, we can prevent them next time and, perhaps, leave a better world.

The *Odyssey* and the *Iliad*

The two books of epic poetry written by Homer are the first works of literature still extant, the two fundamental building blocks of Western writing. For all their study, however, their author is a mysterious figure. About Homer himself, nothing is really known. Tradition says that he was born in Ionia in the eighth century B.C. and that he was an itinerant troubadour known for his verse, but nothing records his own existence until he begins to be mentioned in books written hundreds of years after his. In fact, apart from those handed-down legends, nothing even says that he was one person. It's entirely possible that his books are the works of many, written over generations, drawing on local traditions and tall tales that gradually coalesced into these two giant epic poems. And giant they are. The *Iliad* comprises 15,693 lines; the *Odyssey*, 12,109 lines.

Their stories are timeless, even as they speak of specific historical events. Even though the *Iliad* is a fictionalized literary poem, it's the best account extant of the Trojan War. Helen, the beautiful wife of Menelaus, a king of the Achaeans, has been spirited away by Paris, the son of King Priam of Troy. The Achaeans go after Helen to bring her home, and to avenge her capture, they launch an immense navy to fight the war. As the battle begins, the gods begin to meddle in the battle, the story of which is told in intense detail. It ends, of course, when the Achaean soldiers build a huge wooden horse outside the walls of Troy, which they offer as a gift of peace. The Trojans accept, towing it into the city, whereupon, under cover of night, the soldiers who've concealed themselves inside the horse pour out and conquer the city from within.

In the *Odyssey*, the title character, Odysseus, king of Ithaca, with his crew, is trying to get home after fighting in the ten-year Trojan War. It takes him another decade to get there, and along the way, he encounters strange creatures and dangerous challenges, and his ships are wrecked. The gods alternately help him along and, when angered, impede his voyage. Meanwhile, back at home, several challengers want to marry Odysseus's wife, Penelope, and inherit his estate. They are also plotting to kill his son, Telemachus. When Odysseus gets home, he disguises himself as a beggar, allowing him to assess the situation and come up with a plan to defeat the men who want to take his place. (Only his dog, Argus, recognizes him when he arrives.) Eventually, he confronts them, and they die horrible deaths, whereupon he reveals himself and rejoins his family.

A really amazing number of familiar figures come out of this work. The tale of Jason and the Argonauts is drawn from the *Odyssey*. So, too, the Sirens, the temptresses who drew men to their island with their songs only to entrap them. The popular image of the Cyclops, as a big lumbering creature with one eye in the middle of his forehead, is likewise from the *Odyssey*. More than that, though, generations have been entranced by Homer's beautiful language, both in Greek and in the better translations, most especially the recent version by Robert Fagles. The story of the *Odyssey* is so pervasive that it has given rise to yet another canonical work of literature: James Joyce's *Ulysses*, published in 1922, is a loose retelling of the *Odyssey* through the eyes of a twentieth-century Dubliner.

Aesop's Fables

Like so many of the ancient writers whose works are familiar to school-children, Aesop the man is barely an outline. He was probably born in the sixth century B.C. and is said to have been a freed slave from Samos, though several other places claim him as their own. But his works are another story. Even those without any kind of classical education, who've never read Homer or Aristotle, often know a number of Aesop's fables. That's because these little tales, each ending with a moral lesson, are simple, direct, and memorable—which is why they're so often used to teach schoolchildren.

Take, for example, the fable that might be Aesop's most well known: the story of the tortoise and the hare. The two animals are pitted against one another in a race, which would on the surface seem to be no contest, since the hare is so much more fleet of foot than the tortoise. The hare, convinced that victory is his, dawdles along the racecourse, pausing for a nap, while the tortoise chugs away and defeats the distracted hare. The moral: *Slow and steady wins the race.*

Or the story of the peacock who complained to Juno that he could not sing like the nightingale he so admired. Juno reminded him that he had spectacularly colored feathers and that the fates have assigned something to all. The moral: *Make the best of what has been allotted to you.*

One could go on and list the dozens and dozens of his stories whose lessons remain useful today and whose instructions have become common English expressions: the boy who cried wolf, the ant and the grasshopper, the wolf in sheep's clothing, and so forth. Ironically enough, Aesop's own moral sense led to his personal downfall. In one of the accounts of his life, he came to become an intimate of Croesus, the wealthy king of Lydia. When the king sent Aesop to Delphi to distribute a large quantity of gold to the citizens, he was appalled by their greed and sent the money back to Croesus. (One could see the story as one of his fables' final morals: *If you do not play fair, nobody gets anything.*) However, his attempt to uphold the rules backfired: Aesop was killed by the Delphians. And, in fact, in another twist of history that sounds like a fable, Delphi is said to have been punished soon after by a series of natural disasters.

Sappho

The writings of Sappho exist mostly in tiny fragments. One complete poem and pieces of about one hundred others—quite a few of which contain only four or five words—are all that we have. But her contemporaries, literary and otherwise, knew her work far better than we do. Plato praised her poetry; Solon, the ruler of Athens and a poet in his own right, considered her a genius. She had the good fortune to live on the island of Lesvos, where an artistic community was flourishing, and coming from a prominent family, she was allowed a certain amount of leisure time to write. Lesvos also seems to have been a rather progressive place when it came to women's rights, allowing her talent to evolve. And she was one of the first poets to write about personal experience rather than lofty ideas, especially about love, a subject that makes her work universally approachable. That is compounded by her style: translators often say they have to fight the urge to "decorate" her simple phrasings, clear-eyed view of romance, and direct tone. Consider this snippet, translated by the poet Jim Powell:

In my eyes he matches the gods, that man who
sits there facing you—any man whatever—
listening from close by to the sweetness of your
voice as you talk, the

sweetness of your laughter: yes, that—I swear it—
sets the heart to shaking inside my breast, since
once I look at you for a moment, I can't
speak any longer. . . .

Her subject matter, however, has caused her reputation to suffer through the years. Though she was probably married and had a daughter, it's quite clear from her work that Sappho had a taste for female lovers as well as male ones. Her homosexuality may have contributed to the fact that we don't have much of her poetry today, because medieval scholars disparaged her work and probably didn't spend as much effort copying it and handing it down as they might have. Moreover, she wasn't particularly beloved by the nineteenth-century poets and scholars who otherwise revered the Greeks. It took our era's increased tolerance of homosexuality—as well as our modern taste for more direct and un-ornamented use of language—to revive her reputation. And revived it is: poets today often cite her as a significant influence, and her poems have been repeatedly rendered into English over the past few decades. (J. D. Salinger even used a Sapphic line to title one of his novellas, *Raise High the Roof Beam, Carpenters.*) In the twentieth century, we've also found a few more bits and pieces of her work, some of which turned up on torn scraps of papyrus reused to wrap an Egyptian mummy. One of her lines says it all:

I think that someone will remember us in another time.

As we do.

Zorba the Greek

It begins—like so many Greek things!—in a café. An unnamed narrator, a writer dissatisfied with his life of the mind, is sitting at the port of Piraeus, planning to go and take over a mine in Crete, in hopes that he'll get in touch with his less cerebral side. And into the café walks a figure so vivid and earthy that the narrator is swept up by his gusto. Alexis Zorbas—Zorba—ends up following the narrator to Crete, working as the foreman in the mine, and singing, dancing, eating, drinking, and altogether reveling in the pleasures of life. The narrator, slowly but surely, learns by example. It is a memorable story about how art and experience can change one's life.

The novel of which we speak is, of course, *Zorba the Greek*. Published by Nikos Kazantzakis in 1946 and brought to America a few years later, it has remained an international best-seller ever since. Kazantzakis was a multitalented man, writing plays and poems as well as novels. He translated Dante's *The Inferno* and Goethe's *Faust*. Another of his books, *The Last Temptation of Christ*, is known to many Americans because of its controversial movie version made by Martin Scorsese. He even held a couple of government posts in Greece, serving at one point as Minister of Education and in a position at the United Nations. He even wrote a huge modern sequel to the *Odyssey*, published in 1938 and generally recalled as a difficult and only moderately successful experiment.

But regardless of his other achievements, it is for *Zorba* that he'll chiefly be remembered, for two reasons: First, the book was simply a smash, remaining in print in multiple languages after fifty years. Moreover, to American audiences, it's even better known for the film version directed by Michael Cacoyannis. Though it wasn't particularly well received by the critics on its first release, the movie struck a chord with audiences, in part because it romanticizes Zorba a bit more than the book does, playing up his colorful traits and omitting some of his misogyny. The great English actor Alan Bates plays the buttoned-up narrator, and Anthony Quinn plays Zorba—plays him with such vigor, in fact, that it's the role that continues to define him. Many moviegoers to this day assume wrongly that the actor was himself Greek. (For the record, he was Mexican.)

The other reason for the book's fame is harder to prove, but may be more significant. Right around the time the film of *Zorba* landed in theaters, jet air travel was arriving on the scene. Americans were beginning to see Europe in record numbers, and the Cretan locations on which *Zorba* had been filmed so beautifully looked enticing. Moreover, the unvarnished beauty of Zorba himself held enormous appeal for the hardworking Americans who were likely to travel to Europe—free of inhibition and overwork, and enjoying his life, just as one might wish to do on vacation. In short, and despite some brutal scenes, the film *Zorba the Greek* was the best advertisement for Greek tourism ever produced—right when many people in its audience were newly able to travel overseas for the first time. (Olympic Airways, founded in 1957, capitalized on this new trend magnificently and was responsible for a portion of Aristotle Onassis's fortune.)

And the fact is that Greece today depends on tourism as its principal industry. It's overstating things to say that *Zorba* is responsible. But it's no exaggeration to say that it changed what foreigners thought of Greece and its people forever. Just as Zorba the character remade his narrator's existence for the better, *Zorba* the book (and film) gave Greece itself a new life.

Alexander the Great

He began life destined to be a leader. At the time of Alexander's birth, in 356 B.C., his father, King Philip II of Macedon, was already bringing his land to preeminence among the Greek states. Philip, wanting a supreme education for his son, surely got one: when Alexander was fourteen, the king hired Aristotle himself as a tutor. For the rest of his life, Alexander would idolize Homer, and in fact, the accounts of the Trojan War in the *Iliad* clearly affected his view of military life. (Philip and Alexander also had a classic falling-out when Philip left his teenaged son's mother for another woman; father and son eventually mended their relationship but never fully reconciled.)

And then, at the age of twenty, the prince was thrust into the spotlight: his father was assassinated (at his daughter's wedding!) and Alexander became king. For years, his father had accumulated power with the idea that Macedonia might not only consolidate all of Greece under his rule but also conquer the Persian Empire, at the time the great rival of the Greek Empire. Furthermore, the Greeks resented the Persians because their king of 150 years earlier, Xerxes, had taken so much Greek territory. Alexander set out to regain that land, taking his troops up into Europe and building a base for further operations. Displaying single-minded militarism and a supreme grasp of field tactics, he proceeded with his army into Asia Minor and down toward Syria, resettling the Greek islands that had fallen under Persian control. He returned small towns on the eastern coast of the Aegean to local control, allowing small local democracies to become established. As he pressed on into Asia, the Persians fled eastward, and with the fall of the city of Tyre, a major Persian naval base, Alexander declared himself king of Asia. He was brutal, as was customary at the time; he slaughtered those Persian citizens who did not surrender and sold the women and children into slavery.

And he did not stop there. Alexander pressed on into Egypt, which fell quickly (preferring his rule to that of the Persians), and where he created a new capital, which would bear his name. The city of Alexandria grew fast, and its library was the most significant place of scholarship for the ancient world.

With his victories, Alexander's megalomania developed to a unique degree: he began to think of himself as having been ordained by the gods to succeed and, eventually, as a god himself. (After he took Egypt, an Egyptian priest declared him the son of the Sun God, Amun-Ra.) But even then he continued on, fighting off a last stand by the fading state of Sparta; conquering Babylonia; pressing on to the east through Persepolis, the capital of the Persian Empire, sacking the city and looting its treasury; and then burning down Xerxes' palace to avenge his conquest of Greece. In Persia, Alexander also began to assert his divinity further, requiring his subordinates to bow and address him as a deity.

In the end, his empire would reach India to the east, and his next plans called for extending his power to the west, incorporating present-day Italy and Sicily. The armies of Europe probably would not have stopped him, but, amazingly, a mosquito bite may have done just that: in Babylon, Alexander was struck ill, most likely with malaria. His troops were marched through his rooms to pay their respects to their stricken leader, and on June 13, 323 B.C., Alexander died. He had conquered most of the developed world, and a good portion of the rest, by the age of thirty-two. Nobody who wanted to rule the world—not Charlemagne, not Napoleon, not Hitler—would get so far again.

Spartan Discipline and Courage

It's said that history is written by the victors. So why do the Spartans tend to get short shrift? We remember Athens for its great leaps of intellect and the arts, but Sparta is known for little beyond the severity of its customs. We ought to remember, however, that this military power in fact defeated Athens, lasting in diminished form even after being reconquered by Alexander's Macedonian army, hanging on till long past the heyday of the Greek Empire.

From the beginning, the Spartans were a relentlessly military society, with a strict governmental hierarchy that contrasted with Athens' openness. The Spartans existed to win. A nearby region called "Messenia" (with a much larger population than Sparta) was conquered and enslaved, providing labor to work the farms and leaving every Spartan man available for military service. A newborn Spartan boy who displayed signs of weakness or other lack of fitness was taken outside the city and abandoned to die. The state conscripted healthy boys for their first training at the age of seven; they became soldiers at twenty and stayed in the army until the age of sixty. It was a punishing system, but one that was effective enough that Sparta was one of the few ancient cities not surrounded by a defensive wall.

Even so, however, in the beginning Athens and Sparta fought together to stave off the Persian armies. Their eventual clash, however, known as the Peloponnesian War, essentially destroyed the city-state of Athens. Sparta reigned supreme for well over one hundred years, until the Persian conquest of Greece and then the subsequent empire of Alexander. But it was not finished as a city. Sparta prospered for centuries under Roman rule and beyond until the Goths finished it off in the year A.D. 395.

If Sparta was such a brutal state, what is there to celebrate about it today? In a word: its unmatched discipline and the success that it brought. The Spartans were early proponents of the idea that luxury softened citizens and that an environment without distractions was an environment that produced superior military men. Even the gentler city-states of Greece—which thought the Spartans mad—admired their self-denial and courage. Their manner of living may not exactly be a route to a joyful or artistic existence, but it made Sparta perhaps the most stable of the ancient city-states. And 2,500 years of fighting later, every army in the world seems to agree that severe conditions breed a superior soldier. To this day, even the top officers' quarters in a military installation are invariably described as "spartan."

El Greco

Though the artist known as El Greco is most famous for his images of Spain, especially the city of Toledo, how can the Greeks not take pride in his work? The very name by which he is known (Spanish for "The Greek") tells us how his contemporaries thought of him. And he must have had more than a slight connection to home, since until the very end of his career, he signed his portraits in Greek.

His given name was Domenikos Theotokopoulos, and he was born in Crete (then under Venetian rule) in the 1540s. In his twenties, he moved to Venice itself, then eventually settled in Toledo. He began his career as a painter of church icons, and he learned his lessons well: the elongated faces and tall, lean bodies familiar from Byzantine art heavily influenced his painting for the rest of his life. In Italy, he studied under the great Venetian painter Titian.

He's an odd figure in the history of art. Most artists fit into a sort of time line of their eras, building on the work of their immediate predecessors, forging a style incrementally. Not so El Greco: his paintings look like nothing else being done in the sixteenth century, and little afterward for three hundred years! His sense of perspective is skewed and flattened out in a way that evokes those icons he'd painted as a young man and might be taken at first for a lack of skill. But the reason may have been less habit or awkwardness than a flouting of convention, an artistic device used in order (for example) to crowd extra people into a picture, heightening the sense of drama. That kind of drama was, in fact, a specialty of his: he used lots of strong colors and deep shadows to heighten the theatrical quality, especially in his religious work. A huge painting in the church of Santo Tomé, in Toledo, showing the burial of a count, draws the eye upward into a riot of dramatic activity as angels and saints whisk him upward to meet his Maker.

What art historians know El Greco for, above all, is his skill as a portraitist. His painting of one of his friends, a priest named Fray Félix Hortensia Paravicino, is often regarded as the greatest portrait of its time: the face has personality and life, the flesh is luminous as real skin. One feels, looking at it, that one knows something of the subject—more than just paint on canvas can ordinarily convey.

His unique style, bordering on the bizarre at times, damaged his reputation in the art world for a very long time. Though he had his admirers and even some royal commissions during his life, his work was overshadowed by that of other Spanish painters, especially Velázquez. Only in the late 1800s did his work begin to come back into style, when the Impressionists began to play tricks with perspective that were similar to his. The gradual shift to strong images and undisguised emotion further bolstered his reputation; Cézanne was often compared to him. And the modern artists who followed the Impressionists thought him a genius. Pablo Picasso worshiped him, as did Henri Matisse and even Jackson Pollock. Art historians routinely cite him today as one of the greatest of all Spanish artists—and of Greek ones as well.

Philoxenia

In the early days of the Internet business boom, around 1997 or so, a young New Yorker named Jason Calacanis got into the game. Known around the city for publishing a magazine, *Silicon Alley Reporter*, that covered online businesses, he, like many in his industry, began scheduling conferences where people in the new field could meet, hear lectures, exchange ideas and information, and make deals (all the while paying Calacanis a substantial fee). Many people did the same, usually in hotels or conference centers, but Calacanis's meetings were often more successful, with more repeat business, than the rest. When asked for an explanation, he put it in no uncertain terms: "People were paying a fortune for those other conferences, and they were serving them a few crummy sandwiches. I'm Greek—I knew how to be a *host*."

It's no small distinction, and one that anyone who visits a Greek household for the first time will recognize. The moment you arrive, you are offered a drink, and you'll not see your glass go empty. Within minutes, you'll be offered something to eat. If you decline, don't worry:

you'll get another chance. ("Are you sure? Maybe just some olives and cheese? A little more, yes?") If you're there for dinner, you won't go home without being stuffed to the gills, and you stand a good chance of having a package of leftovers pressed on you as you leave. (Is it any wonder so many Greeks are in the restaurant business?) You are experiencing the uniquely Greek form of hospitality called *philoxenia*.

This is nothing new. In Euripides' play *Alcestis*, the character Admetus has just lost his wife yet welcomes the visiting Herakles into his home, allowing him to throw a party. When Herakles discovers that he's intruded on Admetus's mourning, he's embarrassed, and angrily asks Admetus why didn't he tell him what was going on. Admetus replies that all he has to offer in his grief is his own hospitality. Herakles is touched and immediately forgives him, and the chorus echoes the idea approvingly, here in the translation by Richard Aldington:

> *Even today he opened his house*
> *And received a guest,*
> *Though his eyelids were wet*
> *With tears. . . .*
> *I admire him.*

Greek Light

How can the sunlight in Greece be any different? After all, it is the same sun, and, to a scientist, the light at any similar latitude should be the same. A resident of Seoul, Lisbon, Kansas City, or San Francisco should be bathed in the same rays as a tourist in the Greek islands, right?

But Greeks and visitors alike, for a great many years, have felt otherwise. Repeatedly, in travelogues and stories, they speak of "Greek light" as something special. Artists claim that colors just look different around the Aegean, and for generations they have traveled to Greece to try to capture it on canvas. Poets speak of something magical that this particular brand of illumination does to the landscape. Nikos Kazantzakis put it this way: "In Greece, the light is entirely spiritual." Henry Miller said it penetrated "directly to the soul."

From a scientific standpoint, can the light really vary from place to place? A little bit. As one goes from north to south, the sun's position in the sky changes, and the way light filters through the atmosphere can affect the colors of objects. But among countries in the same part of the world? How can the light in Italy be any different from the light in Greece?

It's all in your perception. Stand on a Greek island, a little crag sticking out of the sparkling Aegean, and what do you see? You see an endless blue sky above and a sparkling field of blue sea below. (Even today, as the Mediterranean nations fight a battle against pollution, the Aegean has stayed remarkably crystalline.) So the sun pouring down from above is reflected back upward from the water, and then it hits the whitewashed buildings, ancient marble structures, and pale limestone cliffs of the Greek landscape. Most of the Greek islands aren't covered in lush dark green, as tropical spots are; they're light in color. Nothing is gray, or even all that dark, and little diffuses the sun's rays. That's especially true in the southern Aegean where it's arid and the sky is often cloudless. The result is dazzling, almost theatrical clarity.

Besides, it's difficult to imagine, in an age of relatively easy international travel, the inviting glow that Greece must have had to a tourist steaming into Piraeus after a lifetime in a foggy, drizzly city like London or Edinburgh. It would've been a revelation, both because of the warm gentle air and because of the seemingly limitless supply of sun. Since Greece was a principal tourist destination for the educated and literary-minded of northern Europe, who hoped to soak up some culture and see the ruins, they would've gone home raving about how everything was different, beginning with the sunlight itself. Those English poets had no idea that they were writing tourist advertising as well as literature, but that's how it worked out.

Greek Dance

Most European countries' folk dances are performed rarely today, just in demonstrations for tourists or in museum-like settings—in other words, they are preserved for posterity but they are no longer living arts. Not so Greek dances. At any wedding or other big celebration (really, anywhere there's a big party), there'll be a moment, especially once the wine starts flowing, when a *santuri* or *bouzouki* sounds. Before you can say "*Opa!*" there's a line of people formed, hands joined, and bodies moving in step. Even novices are encouraged to join in, especially since many Greek dances are simple to perform, and their basics can be picked up in a few minutes. (Even so, newcomers have been known to cause serious disruption in the line.) Traditionally, women and men performed separate dances in separate groups. Those rules are often relaxed today, and many groups are mixed, though some of the more athletic dances are still exclusively male.

Greek dance is believed to have begun in the Minoan culture on the island of Crete, and in fact, Crete remains one of the most dance-happy places in Greece. Before long, in cultures all over Greece there were dancers. Spartans danced before battles; women danced to honor the goddesses; and all sorts of dances were performed at ceremonies like weddings. And quite a number of them look like Greek dances today, in which everyone lines up and joins hands, either snaking around the dance floor or looping around to form a circle. Similarly, hundreds of years later, circle dances led by a powerful citizen were performed throughout the Byzantine world on special occasions, even in the church.

The circle dance, with almost no leaping, is called the *syrto*, which might be the liveliest in Greece and is probably the most widely performed, in all its variations. It got its name from the word meaning a "dragging" or "pulling," and almost all the steps stay close to the floor as the ring of dancers shuffles along slowly and smoothly. The dance is also called a *Kalamatiano*, which suggests that it's from Kalamata, but that's not correct; rather, it's named for a song about a lover's gift of a silk handkerchief, Kalamata having been a well-known silk-producing center in the old days, rather like Como in Italy today. To commemorate that gift, the person who begins the circle takes a piece of fabric, a *mandili*—sometimes a handkerchief, though at a big wedding or a banquet, it's more often a linen napkin—and raises it into the air. The line instantly forms behind the leader, snaking around the dance floor and coming back around to the napkin holder to form a circle. (I once found myself in a circle of *syrto* dancers, barely keeping up, when the fellow next to me departed and abruptly left me holding the napkin, expecting me to lead the dance. The results were not good.) Another popular variation of the *syrto* that's particular to Crete is danced to a slightly different rhythm with more of a kick to the steps.

Even better known is a dance called the *hasapikos*, or "butcher's dance." It gets its name because it was once performed with knives, which were whirled in a series of duel-like movements. (Today the dancers stick to sword-fighting gestures, leaving the actual cutlery out of it.) This very fast-moving dance was once all-male but is now coed. It comes from Constantinople, and its popularity grew in Greece when many ethnic Greeks fled Turkey in the early 1920s. But its real boost came a few decades later, when it appeared in the film *Zorba the Greek*, and for many people who have never seen a Greek dancer in person, it represents the whole genre.

Bouzouki Music

Surprisingly, many non-Greeks draw a blank at the word *bouzouki*. The bulbous little instrument with three or four pairs of steel strings is easily mistaken for a balalaika, a mandolin, or even just some kind of strange guitar. But put on a record of bouzouki music, and it's instantly recognizable. The twangy, metallic sound and the slowly accelerating rhythms are just a little different from everyone else's. It's no wonder that in the movies, bouzouki music invariably accompanies an establishing shot of an island coastline. As thoroughly as the pictures do, the bouzouki screams "Greece."

Interestingly, the bouzouki is a comparatively new invention. Before the early twentieth century, Greek folk bands performed mostly with small accordions and fiddles. But as a new popular-music form called *rebetiko* bloomed in the tavernas around the Aegean, especially in Thessaloniki, the three-stringed, gourd-shaped bouzouki gained popularity. Deeply tied up with Greek national identity, rebetiko music was suppressed by the Turks—a situation that, as with many repressed arts, only made the music more beloved. (It is sort of a Greek analogy to the blues, which served as almost a secret language among American blacks living under slavery and then segregation.) In fact, during the years when rebetiko was officially discouraged, a miniature bouzouki called a *baglamas* evolved; its small size meant it could be hidden away, carried off, or even smuggled into jail as the situation demanded. Today the baglamas is still part of a well-equipped rebetiko band, where its high pitch fills out the upper register.

Like all music fans, bouzouki boosters argue about the greatest performer ever, but many point to Manolis Hiotis, a Thessaloniki native whose discs on Columbia Records brought the instrument's sound to a huge international audience for the first time. He was a technical innovator, the first to build an electric bouzouki, and the man who added a fourth string to the instrument. (A few traditionalists still grumble about that last change, saying that the four-string tuning makes the bouzouki too much like a guitar.)

But the bouzouki is hardly limited to folk music and rebetiko, and here we must mention Mikis Theodorakis. Even if you don't realize it, you've probably heard this composer's music—which often incorporates Greek folk instrumentation—in film soundtracks from *Zorba the Greek* to *Serpico*. He's composed symphonic works and a major piece setting the poems of Odysseus Elytis to music, as well as many operas, several of which draw on ancient sources such as the story of Electra. Just as significant has been his political activity: Theodorakis has served two separate terms in the Greek parliament. He's also been exiled or jailed twice, once for his leftist activities in the 1940s and again after the military junta seized power in Greece in the late 1960s. After each internment, he came roaring back to prominence, debuting new works and new commissions, including a canto especially written for Greece's entry into the European Union and an opera written for the opening of the Olympic Games. He's even built a bridge to his political rivals, serving as a minister in Greece's conservative government of the 1990s.

The Orthodox Church

What defines Greeks as Greeks is not always so simple to pin down. Greece's terrain varies, from sea to mountains; its food, drink, music, and dances all vary by region. But a few things tie the vast majority of ethnic Greeks together, and chief among them is the Greek Orthodox Church. Though there are other religions in Greece, Orthodox Christians constitute well over 95 percent of the population. (At one time, Greece had a substantial number of Jews, but the horrors of the Holocaust and the gentler winnowing of emigration have thinned their numbers greatly. About eight thousand Jews live in Greece today, and within a couple of generations, many of those will likely have intermarried, reducing the practicing Jewish population effectively to zero.) Especially in the years of Italian and Turkish threats to Greek sovereignty, the unifying nature of the church was a powerful force in Greece.

And it has been so for a *very* long time. The Orthodox Church— setting aside the obvious fact that it goes back to the Apostles' worship of Jesus Christ—can be said to have begun in the year A.D. 395, when the dying Roman Empire was carved in half by its emperor, in order that his two sons should rule. The Western half drifted away; the Eastern half, headquartered in the city of Byzantium—later renamed Constantinople, and still later Istanbul—held together for more than 1,100 years, through the reigns of eighty-eight emperors. Even after it ceased to govern the empire, its religious arm held on, becoming the Orthodox Church we know today.

Moreover, it took the form we know fairly early in its history. Power was distributed equally among patriarchates, for example, as it is today, and the structure of the church's administration was set up. (The list of patriarchates has grown over the centuries, but they're still sister churches: Russian Orthodox, Serbian Orthodox, Antiochian Orthodox, and so forth.) Most significantly, the holy scriptures regarding Christ's life were assembled into the volume that we know as the New Testament of the Bible. The remarkable visual arts for which the Byzantine era is known also developed during this era, especially in the ornamentation of manuscripts and icons. Walk into even the most modernist Orthodox church anywhere in the world today, and the murals or mosaics follow particularly defined forms—the figures are tall and thin, with elongated fingers and faces.

I said earlier that the Western half of the Orthodox Church drifted away, but the implication that it faded out of world affairs is far from correct. Through the first several hundred years of the church's existence, the two halves developed several points of friction, chiefly over the place of a supreme individual at the top of the hierarchy. The East wanted a council at the top, headed by a patriarch; the West believed in a pope, a godlike figure on earth. Matters grew worse in the eleventh century, when the two sides issued decrees of condemnation called the "Anathamas." It is hard to date the exact moment the two sides split apart, but most historians call it the Great Schism of 1054. Since then, the Eastern Orthodox churches and the Roman Catholic Church have maintained a badly broken relationship, culminating in the sacking of Constantinople by the West in the fifteenth century. Only in the past generation have church leaders from each side started speaking. The Anathamas, in particular, were lifted in 1965, by mutual consent of Pope Paul VI and Ecumenical Patriarch Athenagoras.

Today there are 250 million Orthodox Christians worldwide. In the melting pot that is the United States, of course, the church is a relatively small minority, with about 5 million members. Of those, 1.5 million are Greek Orthodox. Yet the American arm of the church holds a special place in Constantinople, for its youth and vigor. The archdiocese of America, founded in 1922, is one of the largest outside Greece and, in fact, holds so much wealth and power today that some of its members have asked for its independence as a separate American Orthodox patriarchate. For now, however, its ties to the mother church remain deep.

The Antikythera Mechanism

It is one of the oddest antiquities on earth. In 1901, divers exploring a shipwreck off the Aegean island of Antikythera brought up several bronze and marble statues, as well as several fragments of metal that were too encrusted with oxidation to be easily identified. One of them, on closer examination, turned out to be most of a mechanism filled with gears and rotating plates mounted on a wooden frame. It was marked with lettering that dated the machine to no later than the first century B.C.

Eventually, the machine was cleaned up somewhat and X-rayed, in order to figure out how it was put together. Precise copies were made of the works, and a reconstruction of the machine was assembled. It didn't take long for the researchers' suspicions to be confirmed: the Antikythera mechanism is a sophisticated astronomical clock, indicating the movements of the sun, the planets, and the moon. It is, more or less, a planetarium, one that was likely used for navigation on the sea.

Now, this is very, very strange. We have no record of Greek science (or any early science) going anywhere in the direction of complex instrumentation like this. Moreover, until this machine appeared, the prevailing theory held that the educated ancient Greeks typically ignored applied science: theory was treasured, but practical work was disdained, considered a kind of manual labor. Most puzzling of all, there is nothing else like the Antikythera device for the next thousand years; only around A.D. 1000 do time-recording devices begin to appear in the Arab world and eventually in the Far East. Even the notion of a graduated dial, marked off with numbers or divisions, does not show up for centuries afterward.

And it worked. Once reconstructed, the mechanism operated accurately and smoothly. Moreover, the original works showed signs that they were actually used, not just an experiment: one gear tooth was chipped off and subsequently repaired, as was a spoke in one of the internal wheels. Someone operated this machine often enough that it broke, and they cared enough to fix it.

Who that someone was is still a mystery. Most scholarship traces the shipwreck to the island of Rhodes, which was in fact a center of military and naval technology. It's even been posited that a navigator named Geminus of Rhodes, or one of his followers, was the man behind it, because the inscriptions on the machine are similar to those in Geminus's book, which survives to the present day. (There's also some historical chatter about a far more complex astronomical computer built on Rhodes around the same time, but the evidence of that is very shaky, and of course we don't have the machine itself.) It's even been taken up by a few believers in UFOs and other such ideas, who believe that such sophisticated ancient technology couldn't have arrived any other way except from outer space.

No matter what you believe, the fact of the mechanism's existence is inescapable. Someone in the ancient world was a Leonardo da Vinci of his time, sophisticated in both astronomy and mechanical engineering. Until some future archaeological discovery or scholarship adds to what we know, the best evidence we have points to some smart Greek who wanted to give his compatriots a safe trip home.

Cycladic Art

In the first years of Western civilization—beginning about five thousand years ago, long before the period we think of as Greek—one small corner of Greek culture was already beginning to show its artistic inclination. Off the coast of the Peloponnesian peninsula, the islands known as the Cyclades, especially those around Delos, gave rise to a school of art completely different from what was going on in the rest of the world. (These are the islands near Attica, the peninsula on which Athens sits; the most famous are Mykonos and Santorini.) In Egypt, the art of the pharaohs was reaching new zeniths in realism and giving rise to pyramids and pylons; in Mesopotamia, stylized lions and bearded men were dancing along the palace walls.

But in the Cyclades, artists went in the opposite direction, stripping figures of all but the barest representation of their features. A statue's face was a smooth oval of flawless limestone, with a simple triangular bump to represent the nose; the human body was reduced to a symmetrical, abstracted shape that looks like a violin with a stubby neck. These statues range from a few inches high to life size, and many were once decorated, some with painted-on jewelry. They were produced in great numbers, mostly as funerary figures. Many scholars describe them as fertility figures, though the fact that some are male casts doubt on that idea. (The men are often musicians.)

Of course, Cycladic civilizations produced other artifacts as well. The tombs that yield the figurines also contain pottery, metalwork, and other well-made objects, many decorated with handsome geometric designs, especially spirals. But it's those enigmatic figures that so many people find themselves coming back to, and that's a comment on our world as much as the ancients'. A few generations ago, these artifacts might have been dismissed as artless or even crude—simple aboriginal stuff, like other Bronze Age work. But contemporary eyes see something far more in Cycladic art. Twentieth-century artists' quest for purity of form has opened our eyes to the clean beauty of these figures. A great many modern artists, like Constantin Brancusi, produced sculptures that are extraordinarily similar; the faces in the paintings of Modigliani look very much like Cycladic heads. To put it simply, modern artists were terribly impressed by these works, and no wonder: Cycladic figures (especially today, with the paint scrubbed off) look an awful lot like modern art.

To a certain extent, the parallel is imprecise. The Cycladic sculptors probably didn't have the same intentions as their modernist descendants. They weren't stripping down their ideas to get to their essence; they were still developing those ideas from zero. Moreover, the stream-lined detail on Cycladic figures seems to have developed simply out of pragmatism. These funerary figures were produced in large numbers, and smoothing out the details allowed them to be produced faster and more simply.

Byzantine Art

With all the attention paid to pre-Christian Greek history, it's easy to overlook the great civilization of medieval Greece: the Byzantine era. (What a measure it is of the country's rich history that one can forget a stretch that lasted for one thousand years!) The Byzantine era is usually said to have begun around A.D. 395, when the Roman Empire was split into eastern and western halves. Over the next century, Rome lost much of its international power, leaving the eastern portion of the empire, based in the city of Byzantium—later called Constantinople, and still later Istanbul—as a Christian center.

It was also an artistic center. The Byzantine Empire is best known for metalwork and icons, rendered in diverse materials: ivory, enamel, wood, gold, silver, manuscript vellum, and especially, mosaic tile. The rise of Christianity meant many new churches were being built, and the architectural style of the day called for flat, thin walls and high clerestory windows. Mosaic wall decoration was perfectly suited to decorating those structures, and the sparkle of those thousands of tiny tiles caught the raking light from the windows in spectacular fashion. Even small churches had mosaics covering the domes, the walls, and especially the half-dome over the altar, often treated with an image of Christ with his hands raised, embracing the congregation.

To an uneducated eye, much medieval art looks amateurish compared with its Greek and Roman predecessors. The Greek statue's gorgeous musculature, for example, disappears in the later centuries, replaced by much more angular renderings of the human body. The paintings and mosaics in Byzantine churches look flatter and less natural than their Classical Period forebears. This point of view was held by Edward Gibbon, the author of the definitive eighteenth-century work, *The Decline and Fall of the Roman Empire*, and it still gets some believers to this day. But it was not a loss of skill or civilization that brought about the change, for the style of art produced by early Christians began to change while the Roman Empire was still intact.

What happened was not a breakdown but a "denaturing"—that is, movement toward a style in which artists weren't trying to reproduce exactly what they saw. Instead, they were trying to express their faith, to instruct and affect the viewer in powerful new ways. Byzantine mosaicists, especially, tend to be unfairly tagged as less sophisticated artists than their Roman predecessors. For one thing, their work is often on ceilings and high walls, and larger, sparklier tiles were necessary to produce strong effects on viewers at floor level. For another, mosaic tends to reward bold forms—it's much less a medium of tone and shading than painting is. The hands in these images are unnaturally long and narrow, for example, but not because the artists couldn't produce them accurately—it was to draw them out, to suggest ethereal grace and delicacy. The so-called crudeness of Byzantine art is a move toward artistic sophistication, even if it sometimes looks like the opposite.

Byzantine culture produced many monuments that survive to this day—several beautifully decorated buildings at Ravenna, Italy, a spectacular church full of mosaics in Sicily, and the eleventh-century Church of the Theotokos at Hosios Loukas in Greece. But one must take a moment here to talk about Hagia Sophia, built for the Emperor Justinian in Constantinople starting in the year A.D. 532. Hagia Sophia ("hagia," pronounced "eye-yah," is Greek for "saint") is a monumental building with a huge dome at its apex, 108 feet in diameter—one of the largest ever constructed before the age of steel. Although much of its ornament inside was treated badly over the years and is now damaged or obscured, one of its chief qualities is unmistakable: Around the edge of the dome, between the ribs that support it, there's a ring of small arched windows. The light streaming in creates a glowing ring around the dome's base, making it look for all the world as if the dome is floating. To a medieval pilgrim, already awed by the space, it must have seemed as if God himself were immediately overhead.

Hagia Sophia has been through a lot over the centuries. As a piece of engineering, it's somewhat flawed: that enormous dome was inadequately supported from the start, and buttresses have been piled up next to it over the centuries to beef up the structure. (It's somewhat of a miracle that Turkey's frequent earthquakes haven't shaken it to the ground.) In the fifteenth century, at the fall of Constantinople to the Ottoman Turks, the city became Islamic, and Hagia Sophia was converted into a mosque. Four minarets were added, and much of the interior decoration was painted over or removed, replaced with Arabic script. And—mirroring the region's history even further—in the twentieth century, the building was deconsecrated, becoming a museum. Since then, a slow archaeological project is uncovering some of the remaining Byzantine works inside.

The other great Byzantine monument is the church of St. Mark's in Venice. A huge cleaning and restoration in recent years has revealed the mosaics and other details in all their glory, and a visitor can now see the complex iconography of this church in full flower. Built in the 1250s, St. Mark's again does spectacular things with light—much of the mosaic tile is golden and reflective—and for the unlettered masses who worshiped here eight hundred years ago, it was as much a teaching aid as an inspiration. The Evangelists are pictured writing their gospels; Christ ascends to the heavens; and the Old Testament is recounted on the outside of the church, with the New Testament inside. It is a spectacular example of another Byzantine quality: that of art as education. The point of all this work was to teach faith to the citizenry, most of whom were illiterate. And walking into St. Mark's is like walking into an illuminated manuscript.

That tradition continues, in modified form, to the present day.

Most Greek Orthodox churches today, even those styled with modernist severity, draw on Byzantine art. The domes usually incorporate a mosaic of Christ as Pantocrator, the first three fingertips of his right hand touching, in the gesture still used by Orthodox priests as they bless the congregation.

The Olympic Games

Then as now, they would gather every four years, the best athletes sent by their hometowns to compete for the highest honors in sports. They would oil their bodies, stretching in the sun, luxuriating in the attention, and flirting (and sometimes doing more) with the hangers-on who came to watch them. At the opening ceremonies, their names were called, one by one, as they paraded out of a stone tunnel into the stadium, to cheers. The best of the athletes were national celebrities, and they would enter to a roaring crowd that at its peak swelled to forty thousand people.

It does not sound profoundly different from a modern sporting event, aside from the oiling-up part (and bodybuilders still do that). The ancient Olympic Games, in fact, are very much the template for modern athletic tournaments. Classical Greece at its height, like today's first-world countries, was completely mad for sports and embraced the cult of the healthy body, not only for its vigor but out of those familiar ideas of objective beauty. At the Games, you had a muscular young man doing what his muscles were perfectly trained for. That was, to the Greeks, something to behold, and a great many fans today would agree.

The Olympics were also an earthy, pagan event, replete with animal sacrifices. All the athletes competed naked; married women were barred from the stadium, although they could probably watch from across the river. The Games began small, in 776 B.C., at the instruction of the Oracle of Delphi, a festival proclaimed to appease the gods during a plague. The first Games had only one event, a footrace; the winner was a fellow named Coroibos, from the nearby city of Elis. Elis, in fact, would go on to be the permanent host city for the Games, controlling the stadium operations and housing many athletes, coaches, and spectators. But, of course, the Games themselves were held at the stadium in Olympia, giving them their name. (Incidentally, Olympia, which is down in the Peloponnese, should not be confused with Mount Olympus, the traditional home of the gods in northern Greece.) The governments of Greece's various city-states were so enamored of the event that they would, every four years, declare a halt to any battles that were going on, in an event called the "Olympic Truce."

As the popularity of the Games grew, so did the list of events. Boxing and equestrian events (along with the very popular, if bloody, chariot race) made their debut. So did the pentathlon, which would eventually become the most celebrated of the track-and-field events, incorporating the javelin, discus, long jump, sprinting, and wrestling. (The stone threshold that marked the starting line still survives, undisturbed, and if you go to Olympia, you are welcome to have a run on the ancient course yourself.) Other races were added to the program, including a three-mile distance race called the *dolichos*. The victors took home no medals, but they were awarded olive wreaths at the closing ceremonies. In the evenings, huge banquets were followed by even huger parties, at which drinking and carousing were not only commonplace but expected. Courtesans were known to take home an entire year's wages from Olympic Week.

The Games probably peaked in 476 B.C., during the brief moment when a unified Greece had just defeated the Persian armies, Periclean Athens was at its peak, and the facilities at Olympia had just been renovated and expanded. Unfortunately, it wasn't going to last. Within a few decades, the Peloponnesian Wars would pit the city-states against each other, and the golden age of Athens would end. But the Olympics still continued for a very long time, through the Roman era and beyond. The final official Games took place in A.D. 393; the following year, the emperor Theodosius I banned all pagan festivals. A few years later, his successor ordered the Temple of Zeus at Olympia—the centerpiece of the Games, even more than the stadium—burned to the ground. The Games were over, after a run of 1,200 years.

Except that they weren't forgotten. In the late nineteenth century, the educated men of Europe were completely besotted with the classical world, and especially with ancient Greek idealism. In 1892, a French baron named Pierre de Coubertin announced that he planned to reestablish the Olympic Games, and subsequently created a committee to arrange them. The first modern Games were inevitably assigned to

Greece and took place in Athens, in 1896. Events were created to evoke the spirit of the ancient Games, such as the revived discus and javelin throws. And a new footrace, the marathon, was invented, to commemorate Pheidippides' fabled run from Marathon to Athens. Fourteen countries participated, mostly from northern Europe; an American named James Connolly won the first modern medal, in the triple jump, and a German, Carl Schumann, won in three different sports. (Women weren't a part of those Games, though they arrived four years later, in 1900, for one event—tennis—and began to be admitted in a substantial way in the 1920s.)

Everyone knows what has happened since then. The modern Olympic Games is the largest sporting event in the world, involving billions of dollars and, in recent years, about ten thousand athletes. And in 2004, they came home again to Athens, but not without a little excitement. Modern Greece has a reputation for being a little lackadaisical about planning and executing public works, and a rather cavalier attitude toward deadlines had early on pervaded the planning for the Games. At one point, the International Olympic Committee grew so nervous that its president threatened the Greeks with the loss of the Games, which would have been an unequaled international humiliation. The Greeks pulled it together in the nick of time, as they so often have, finishing the stadium a few weeks before the athletes came marching in and managing a splendid event, unmarred by failures of infrastructure or security.

An interesting side note: one thing the crowds did not see either at the ancient Games or in 1896 was the lighting of the Olympic flame. The setting ablaze of a torch at Olympia (using the sun's rays, focused by parabolic mirrors borne by young women wearing white tunics) is, surprisingly enough, a relatively modern creation and one that comes from an ugly historic moment. Though the lighting of the flame began at the 1928 Olympic Games in Amsterdam—the same year that the Parade of Nations took its current form, with Greece entering first and the host nation last—the ceremony got a huge boost at the notorious 1936 Games in Berlin. Adolf Hitler was transfixed by the idea and threw a huge amount of backing behind the principle that a flame could be borne from Olympia to Berlin by runners—Aryan runners, of course, representing his Master Race. After the fall of Nazi Germany, the relay continued and, in a delicious irony, has become a celebration of the world's diversity, routed through as many nations and carried by as wide a variety of people as can possibly be arranged. It is testimony to the power of the Olympic movement that a twisted and divisive idea has become one of the planet's most stirring expressions of international brotherhood—probably the closest thing to an Olympic Truce that our messy modern world can achieve.

Worry Beads

You are in a café or on a bus or waiting for an appointment in any city in Greece, and you hear it from the next seat: *Click-click. Click-click. Click-click.* You turn to see where it's coming from, and someone— young or old, rich or poor, but usually male—is performing one of the most definitively Greek actions there is: he's fiddling with a set of *komboloi*, or worry beads. Handling a circle of cord or chain loosely strung with a dozen or so beads and ending in a tassel is a national habit, as much as arguing about politics or smoking too much. And although other cultures around the Mediterranean have vaguely similar tradi- tions—Muslim prayer beads and Catholic rosaries look faintly like worry beads—the act of semi-mindlessly flicking your way through an endless loop of *komboloi* doesn't really translate to anywhere else.

Who knows, those other strings of beads may have given birth to the *komboloi*, or the Greeks may have been there first; their origin is not well understood. It's possible, at least, that the prayer beads held by Greek Orthodox monks became secularized and took the form we know today. Whatever their early history, however, it's clear that they emerged in the eighteenth century, and by the early 1900s were firmly established all over Greece. They are a national quirk, and a useful one: in a culture devoted to argument and café-sitting, after all, the soothing effect of a small, repetitive manual activity is rather profound. At one time, *komboloi* were exclusively a male habit, though today quite a few women carry them as well; Melina Mercouri, ever the trendsetter, was perhaps the first woman in public life to do so.

Their function aside, many sets of *komboloi* are also gorgeous objects in and of themselves. The beads are made from every conceivable kind of material: glass, stone, plastic, wood. Today they come in every color, though traditionalists tend toward a particular set of orangey yellow tones. (That may be because some of the most prized worry beads are made from nearly transparent Baltic amber, which naturally occurs in that color.) The sets that are strung on a fine metal chain last longer and make a lovely jingly sound as one fingers the beads; the ones with a silken cord move more smoothly and are, arguably, more restful. The various materials from which the beads are made produce a variety of sounds as they clack together. *Komboloi* also come in a variety of sizes: some sets are barely six inches long and are kept in a pocket, while others are more than a foot long, with a great big tassel, and usually serve as decorative items for the wall. And if you, the reader, are yourself a Greek American, the chances are better than not that a set is hanging on a doorknob somewhere in your house right now.

The Parthenon

It seems impossible, when you first visit Athens: you look up and *there it is*, the Acropolis, a buttressed mountain rising smack in the middle of a sprawling metropolis. Its crown jewel, visible from all sides by day, flood-lit by night, is one of the most recognizable monuments in history.

The Parthenon, completed in 432 B.C., was built as a temple to Athena, the patron deity of Athens (*Parthenos* means "virgin," referring to the goddess). It also served as a treasury for the city at the height of its golden age of wealth and power, housing coins, jewelry, armor, and other valuables. Interestingly, it is unclear who the architect was: different ancient sources variously name Iktinos, Kallikrates, and Karpion.

The sculptor Phidias is believed to have overseen the decoration of the pediments with magnificent, larger-than-life-size statues, as well as the colossal gold-and-ivory representation of Athena that stood at the temple's center. Though modern eyes see beauty in the severe white Pentelic marble, the temple was originally painted blue and red and filled with metal ornamentation so that it shimmered with color. Even in its ruined state, the Parthenon awes thousands of visitors each year with its majestic air of unity and grace.

The basic proportions of the building are repeated (width to height, column spacing to column height, and so forth) to achieve its unique harmony, pleasing to the eye from every angle. The architects refined the traditional Doric order to perhaps its ultimate level and even applied sophisticated optical tricks to the eight columns across the front and back and seventeen along each side. For example, the columns along the east and west ends of the building are irregularly spaced, paradoxically making them appear even. The outer columns tilt inward ever so slightly, to make the building seem more imposing from the ground.

The Parthenon survived the centuries as a religious building, becoming at various times a Byzantine church, a Catholic church, and even a mosque with a minaret. Its exterior remained largely intact until 1687. That's when occupying Turks, fighting off the Venetian army, used the building to store ammunition. A stray Venetian shot fell through the roof, ignited the powder, and blew out much of the eastern side of the building, damage that remains obvious today.

In 1801, the monument fell prey to a different kind of indignity: Britain's Lord Elgin, acting to save what he felt were imperiled treasures, ordered nearly all the statuary and reliefs pried from the building and shipped to London, where they remain a controversial exhibit at the

British Museum. Greece has repeatedly demanded them back, and Britain has repeatedly refused. Recently, the official British line has softened—Prime Minister Tony Blair at one point came out in favor of the marbles' return—and it seems entirely possible that they will head home in the decades to come.

The Sea

Homer called it "the wine-dark sea," and in certain wintry weather, he is right: it can appear nearly black and foreboding, and surely an ancient naval warrior, thinking of future battles and the very real possibility of his death, might see it in the bleakest possible terms. But the Aegean is most of all not green and not gray like the North Atlantic but blue—impossibly azure in the summer sun, when it sparkles like few other parts of the ocean. (The Caribbean, with its white-sand floor, is similar.) The pale heaps of stone that constitute the Aegean islands rise from the blue; bleached in the sun, they turn almost white, helped along by the builders of houses and businesses, who whitewash their stucco walls, providing a pure background for the color of the water.

The sea, to Greeks ancient and modern, provided (and continues to provide) food, business opportunity, and transportation. The Greeks who lived in the mountains on the mainland were landlocked and far poorer than their coastal and island fellows; no wonder so many of the

Greek myths involve island-hopping. (Not to mention Poseidon, who lives there.) It is bound up in national identity to a degree unmatched anywhere else, and for this bold assertion there is proof. The Greek flag, and the logo of nearly every Greek company or other institution world-wide, is blue and white.